Homo Domesticus

Homo Domesticus

NOTES FROM A SAME-SEX MARRIAGE

DAVID VALDES GREENWOOD

Da Capo

LIFE
LONG

A Member of the
Perseus Books Group

Copyright © 2007 by David Valdes Greenwood

Some of the content in this work appeared in different form in the
"Coupling" column of *Boston Globe Magazine* from 2004–2006.
Some passages have been adapted from my weekly column, also titled
"Homo Domesticus," which appeared in *Bay Windows* in the late nineties.

Epigraph from *Nothing Personal* © 1964 by James Baldwin. Copyright renewed.
Collected in *The Price of the Ticket,* published by St. Martin's.
Used by arrangement with the James Baldwin Estate.

Designed by Trish Wilkinson
Set in 11.5-point Garamond MT by the Perseus Books Group

Library of Congress Cataloging-in-Publication Data

Greenwood, David Valdes.
    Homo domesticus : notes from a same-sex marriage / David Valdes
Greenwood. — 1st Da Capo Press ed.
       p.   cm.
    ISBN-13: 978-0-7382-1081-0 (hardcover : alk. paper)
    ISBN-10: 0-7382-1081-1 (hardcover : alk. paper) 1. Greenwood, David
Valdes. 2. Same-sex marriage—United States—Case studies. 3. Gay
men—United States—Biography. 4. Gay fathers—United States—
Biography. 5. Gay adoption—United States—Case studies. I. Title.
HQ1034.U5G74 2007
306.874'2086640973—dc22   2006030184

First Da Capo Press edition 2007

Published by Da Capo Press
A member of the Perseus Books Group
http://www.dacapopress.com

Da Capo Press books are available at special discounts for bulk purchases in the
U.S. by corporations, institutions, and other organizations. For more information,
please contact the Special Markets Department at the Perseus Books Group,
11 Cambridge Center, Cambridge, MA 02142, or call (800) 255-1514 or
(617) 252-5298, or e-mail special.markets@perseusbooks.com.

1 2 3 4 5 6 7 8 9

For Jason and Lily:
my true loves

"The sea rises, the light fails, lovers cling to each other, and children cling to us. The moment we cease to hold each other, the moment we break faith with one another, the sea engulfs us and the light goes out."

—*James Baldwin*

Contents

A Threat to Marriage?

Where Babies Come From

Hello, Young Lovers

1

Why We Marry

THERE ARE MYRIAD REASONS WHY TWO PEOPLE MIGHT marry—sudden pregnancy, desire for a green card, federal benefits—but only two good reasons to have a wedding: so that you may shamelessly solicit presents and so that you can make people cry.

When I look back on my wedding day, I do not think of the controversy that was already swirling around the topic of gay marriage, even in 1995. I do not pause to consider whether my vows that day began the inexorable decline of our society, as preachers kept implying. And I don't actually think about all the swag we got from friends and relatives simply for saying "I do." No, I think about how this blessed event reduced very old, very cranky people to tears.

Our wedding was to be on New Year's Day, 1995. My husband-to-be, Jason, still had a few living grandparents who would attend, and Grampa Greenwood, the patriarch of Jason's clan, was just about the least likely person you could imagine ever being involved in a gay wedding. I had never met him before the eve of our big day, and I can't say that I was initially looking forward to the prospect.

Irascible, tart-tongued, and somewhat immune to the emotional frailty of others, Grampa had been quite a figure in Jason's childhood. With cultural opinions that can be most charitably described as vintage, Grampa had at one time or another bad-mouthed just about every category of person he did not himself belong to, including gays. Of course, it's easy to let invective fly when you don't know your grandson really *is* a sissy.

But Grampa Greenwood was no caricature either. That November, when Jason and I had announced we wanted to get married on New Year's Day in Boston (not considering the scramble for air and hotel reservations that would ensue), Grampa did not hesitate: he immediately booked himself a flight from Arizona and a hotel room in Copley Square. On the day before his flight, when he asked us to pick him up at the airport, he was in fine form already, declaring, "I'll be the one in a cowboy hat!" That's right, we weren't to look for the face that I knew had loomed over Jason throughout his entire youth—we were to look for a cowboy hat. And so we did.

The next day, there he was, hat towering above the crowd around the Delta desk, and he looked damn pleased with himself. During the cab ride to his hotel, he did most of the talking, cheerfully referencing people of color and women's anatomy in language typically poo-pooed by us uptight East Coast liberals. I glanced a little nervously at the cab driver to see what he thought of this colorful stream of conversation, but it was clear Grampa's speech hardly qualified as a revelation to a Boston cabbie. When we dropped Grampa off, he made a point to tell us that he hoped we'd be okay with him leaving his hat on during our wedding. "A real cowboy," crowed this former insurance man from Connecticut, "never takes off his hat."

The morning of the wedding, he hosted a Greenwood Family Brunch, a family tradition. At brunch, his cowboy hat was indeed on, which distinguished him as the head of the table, around which crowded a stereotype-defying blend of business-savvy Republicans and former hippie potters. I sat among them, sipping my mimosa, happy to revel in all the attention. I know that sounds shallow, but come on: wallflowers don't have weddings; they elope. Weddings are designed *specifically* so other people will fawn over you all day. I was ready for some high-grade fawnage, and Jason's relatives were happy to do the honors.

My own family would never provide such a thing. It's not that they weren't loving people. It's just that their first love was a rather scary version of God, heavy on the Old Testament and not a bit down with sodomites. I grew up Seventh-day Adventist, a faith I describe as soft-core fundamentalist: they take the Bible literally but don't picket AIDS patients' funerals. Applying the old saw of "love the sinner but not the sin," which makes them loving and me a sinner, my family could claim to love Jason and me without coming to our wedding. While Jason's family members were filling themselves with French toast and eggs Benedict at Boston's Copley Hotel, mine were far away, wondering how I could have fallen so far.

I had known it would be this way. I had come out to everyone else in my life long before I ever told my mother. A single parent who had raised two boys while battling poverty, depression, and lupus, she'd grown ever more faithful to the church as she grew older and her life got harder. As close as we had always been, I'd had a pretty clear vision of her reaction to the idea of a flaming homosexual son and—sissy that I am—I waited to tell her until she broached the subject.

It was Thanksgiving Day, just over two years before my wedding, and I was home from Emerson College, where I was doing graduate work. Home was Norridgewock, Maine, a town of "3,000 friendly people," at least according to the optimistic sign that welcomes you as you descend onto the tiny Main Street. As far back as my memory goes, my family had lived in my grandparents' colonial-era house on Upper Main Street, except for several brief intervals when my mom had found cheap HUD apartments for the three of us to live in on our own.

By the time I came out, my grandfather was long dead, but Grammy was still—and I will be gentle here—the opinionated woman she had always been. Only her hearing was failing; she sat close to the television that Thanksgiving night, so as not to miss a single vowel on *Wheel of Fortune*. Across the room, stuffed into easy chairs, Mom and I were talking about a queeny old man in her church. She suggested he might still someday marry, and I snorted that he was pretty content in his closet, lined as it was with velvet drapes and costly antiques.

"You seem to know so much about it; do you have a closet to come out of?" she asked, eyes bright and expression playful. Having vowed never again to lie about my sexual identity, I responded, "Only at home." Her face froze, a dot of pink appearing on each white cheek. As she fell silent, I could hear on the television a well-chosen letter occasioning a series of dings and audience applause. (Let me just say, there's something perversely, satisfyingly all-American about coming out during

Wheel of Fortune.) When Mom finally managed to speak, it was a whisper through tight lips. "If I'd thought the answer was yes, I wouldn't have asked the question."

That night began a slow dance of rejection and acceptance that became a pattern. She didn't speak to me for weeks, and when she finally picked up the phone to call, she made it clear that, though she couldn't accept the gayness, she wanted me back in her life. Meanwhile, I was to swear never to tell Grammy, whose weak heart would officially expire at the news.

My grandmother, a woman who should never have been underestimated, was listening to this entire conversation on the other phone. Annoyed that anyone would dare try to keep her in the dark, she bypassed my mother and sent me a letter in which she sniffed that nobody had to tell her I was gay. "I may be old but I'm not stupid," she wrote in the tender voice for which she was known. After making it clear that she believed that this was a phase and reminding me that she loved me even so, she closed with this brilliant p.s.: "Time is short and Satan desires every one of us." Yes, my grandmother could take her loving guilt-trip all the way to the apocalypse.

Meanwhile, my mother was alternating between saying the wrong things—like "My prayer group is praying you out of it!"—and trying to show a comfort with things she perceived as gay: "Have you seen that RuPaul? I just love him!" But theoretical acceptance of an enormous drag queen is very different from acceptance of one's practicing homosexual son. When I started seeing Jason seriously in the fall of 1993, and had the audacity to talk about this with her, it was a development she could not accept. She made it clear he was not invited home with me.

I, in turn, made it clear that if he wasn't welcome, I wasn't making the trip north either. That winter, the months without seeing me passed slowly for my mother and grandmother. By the summer of 1994, they couldn't stand my absence anymore; then, in a nifty bit of emotional timing, my grandmother had a teeny little heart attack, just big enough to offer Mom an excuse to summon me—and Jason—home. I wouldn't say my grandmother faked the attack to get me up there, but I will point out that when Jason and I arrived the next morning, she was wearing shorts and pulling up weeds in her garden. To our relief, after a frosty welcome, both Mom and Grammy took to Jason so much that they started hounding us to agree to spend Thanksgiving with them.

Thanksgiving is only five weeks before New Year's Day, mind you. Considering how my grandmother beamed with pride as Jason kept eating and eating and eating, and how my mother hugged us both tight before we left, it would seem reasonable to expect that they would have considered attending our wedding just over a month later. But Thanksgiving is not an institution created by God himself in a leafy garden and thus can't really be desecrated by same-sex pie eaters. A holiday dinner was fine, but we could think again if we imagined them tossing any rice on our big day.

This position reflected my grandmother's firm beliefs about marriage, many of which she had outlined to me over the years. She believed that her eldest daughter had had too many marriages and her youngest daughter too few. She told me that divorce was reprehensible unless the husband was a pervert, in which case all bets were off. And she was convinced that new towels from Renee's department store were the only wedding gift worth giving, which is why nearly every relative and friend who married received a set with her compliments. But nothing in all her years of experience allowed for marriage to involve fewer than one woman and more than one man. Our wedding would be a mockery of a sacred institution.

Frankly, this cut-and-dry opinion was no surprise; both from the faith I was raised in and from what I had seen in the media, I had grown up expecting that rejection was all a homosexual could rationally expect from this world. But, damn the old rules and my family's adherence to them, plenty of others were determined to prove that notion wrong.

When the day came, I called home and let my mother know that twenty-eight of Jason's relatives from eight states, including two elderly grandparents, would be celebrating our union. Jason's mother, Nancy, I pointed out, who hated to be up in front of people, was planning to begin our ceremony by walking to the front of the chapel to pin boutonnieres on our vests. I told my mom that it would hurt terribly when I looked through the assembled crowd for my own family and their faces were absent. When my mother started to protest that this was unfair, I said I didn't have time to argue about this because I had a brunch to go to—which, by the way, may be the gayest possible way to cut short a conversation.

Just an hour later, as I found myself surrounded by enthusiastic future in-laws, I had a perspective shift of soul-stirring proportions: this was proof that we didn't have to settle for the cold shoulder, that we could bask in the warm embrace of family. With so much love around me, it's no wonder I felt so relaxed. Or perhaps it was the second mimosa. I'm a good former fundamentalist, which is to say, an alcohol lightweight—two mimosas can do me in.

As Jason and I bid good-bye to the brunch set, we didn't especially hurry to get to the Arlington Street Church, in whose tiny chapel we'd be tying the knot less than two hours later. It was cold, but no blizzard had materialized—a peril of planning a winter wedding in Boston—so we enjoyed our walk, taking time to enjoy the ice sculpture displays left over from the city's New Year's Eve celebration.

When we rang the church doorbell, a rumpled man in a dirty T-shirt and jeans answered the door. It was the church prior we'd been required to hire for the service. "Sorry," he said, "I was in the fridge." Literally, inside the unit, fixing it. It hadn't occurred to Jason and me that the guy who'd be letting in all our guests would also be doing the church's repairs. It was our first taste of the unpredictability of even the most perfectly planned wedding.

Our friend Lee Anna, whose own wedding had been a massive extravaganza of pink fabric and soap bubbles, had given us one piece of advice: expect at least one thing to go completely wrong on your wedding day. Count on the likelihood that something you can't predict will get screwed up, and then, when it does, just roll with it. When it happens, say to yourself, "This is the thing that was supposed to go wrong." Get over it on the spot and then tell it as a story someday.

The prior in hobo attire was not "the thing" Lee Anna warned us about. Nor was the circus-train speed with which the pianist would soon play Bach's Prelude in C Major from the Well-Tempered Clavier, requiring our attendants to hurry down the aisle like contestants in a speed-walking race. (To the pianist's credit, this apparently was a historically accurate tempo, but we'd only heard the kinder, gentler version favored by children at recitals.) "The thing" wasn't even the family of five complete strangers who would later attend our wedding reception because the restaurant owner couldn't bear to turn them away, thus providing three very young children with an informal education in progressive causes.

No, "the thing" that went wrong was this: I forgot my pants.

It's not as if I was actually naked, attending my own wedding in (shudder) a thong. It's just that I was still dressed for brunch in an outfit that was more casual, less poet-gone-wild than my intended wedding ensemble. The black jeans—here let me pause to shake my head: *black jeans?*—I had worn to brunch were just fine in a hotel restaurant, but they'd never do for, say, a wedding, especially not for the groom. Either of them.

We did not discover this little snag the moment we walked through the door. We arrived at the chapel exactly one hour before the wedding, because that was all the church would allow us for rehearsal. Six of our friends were there, ready to practice being attendants—not bridesmaids, since one of them had a penis—along with the pianist and a friend who would deliver the homily. We were a boisterous bunch, and our laughter echoed off the tiled marble floors and Tiffany stained-glass windows.

Now, I'm a bit of a control freak, I admit. I like to plan and to oversee the execution of my plans. But on this day, I was feeling so smug—I did it! I pulled it off!—that I let the conversation roll on a bit instead of immediately forcing everyone into their places, which would normally be my inclination. "A bit" means I graciously waited a full fifteen minutes—and that is a lot of time for a control freak—before finally marshalling everyone into order. We'd lost a quarter of all the time we had before I had us walking through who would stand where and do what.

I cannot recall what it was that made me think of my wedding outfit. There is a photo of me at just about that moment, clad in jeans and issuing orders, with a tense look on my face. Somehow it hit me: I have no pants. I could clearly picture my white silk poet shirt (did I mention it was the nineties?) on its hanger in the church restroom, along with the brocade wedding vest made with love by Nana, Jason's grandmother on his mother's side. Just as clearly, I could see my wedding pants laid out on a chair in my Somerville apartment, two towns away. The wedding was to be at three o'clock and it was two twenty when I ended the rehearsal, hurling myself into the car of the lone male attendant, heading pantsward.

Neal had been my friend since college and was the first straight guy I had ever told I was gay. I had made quite a drama of the thing, coming out during my last semester in a seven-page letter that I sealed in an envelope and handed to Neal; then I sat stricken at his side while he read my assurances that he had nothing to fear from me and blah blah yakkedy yak on. Poor guy: he later told me it took every ounce of reserve he had not to laugh out loud. Not at my orientation, but at my pathetic, abashed state. Flash forward to my wedding day and his task was to keep me calm. "We have plenty of time," he assured me, maneuvering off Beacon Street and onto Storrow Drive, an often-clogged route that was—thank you, televised bowl games!—nearly empty of traffic that afternoon.

As if we'd been teleported, we were at the door of my apartment just a few minutes later. Jason and I lived three floors up in a slope-walled attic that had been optimistically billed as a two-bedroom unit after the landlord threw up two divider walls in the space. As I hurried up the stairs, rising above the clouds of pot smoke that surrounded the landlord's first-floor unit, I unbuckled my belt and tried to climb even while removing my jeans. This was an ungainly trick, and when I opened the door to our place, I toppled into the room, one leg still in the jeans. Once I had that leg free, I grabbed the wedding pants and, having learned nothing, attempted to put them on while descending.

I did have a brief vision of falling, and I imagined the mortification of lying there half out of my pants, possessed of a secondhand buzz, as the paramedics found me. But I made it to the car without incident, and soon we were flying up the street.

A man in such a hurry ought to have singular vision at this point, right? Think again. As we careened up Massachusetts Avenue—it was now twenty minutes before the wedding—I happened to glance out the window at the restaurant where we would later be holding our reception. We had asked for things to be kept simple: white tablecloths, which a friend would adorn with single strands of orchids. But, as we drove by, I caught a glimpse through the restaurant windows of something I simply could not abide: the linens alternated table by table, red then white then red, with the next row reversing the pattern. It looked like an ad for Prince spaghetti night.

"Stop the car!" Something in my voice must have made it clear that I actually meant this, and Neal pulled over just a block after my cry. I ran to the restaurant and paused at the door, not bothering to enter. I simply shouted in at the owner, "I said white!" He looked around at his improvisation, shrugged, and said, "This is festive!" Sounding petulant and commanding all at once, I bellowed back, "White!" He flashed me his charming smile. "It'll be white."

Meanwhile, as I was barking instructions through the restaurant door, Jason was back at the church, clad in his wedding finery and trying not to vomit. Jason, like his mother, does not like to be in front of a crowd. He's a family person and appreciates ritual, so a wedding made sense to him, but he is not a performer, and the very thought of being one of the two stars of this show made him want to hurl. That had been true even when he thought I would be there to calm him down; it was now exacerbated by the fact that it was ten minutes before our wedding and I was nowhere in sight, leaving him to do all the greeting.

This was not Jason's idea of a good time. Consider another day, just seven months earlier, when the spotlight was also to be on him. It was the day of his first professional presentation during a grad student internship. Knowing he was nervous, I walked with him to the train, but we hadn't gotten far when he stopped in his tracks to discreetly toss his cookies. While that kind of stage fright has since lessened to a great extent, it was still in play at the time of our wedding. And if there was anything more nerve-wracking than the thought of us being in front of everyone together, it was the hurlworthy possibility of him being in front of everyone alone.

Jason's fear of being trapped in the spotlight has a companion trait in his emotional encounters: not at all prone to big emotional displays, he hates being under the gun to provide them. If I waited a million years, he would never make a big gooey declaration of his feelings for me, *especially* if he knew I was waiting for one. He is perfectly content to let me be the Grand Gesture person, while he is more the Quiet Proof guy. He has no problem being openly loving, but likes to display this in his own eminently practical ways. Despite my sometimes embarrassingly romantic nature, I love him for this. In fact, my first inkling that I should keep him around for a while came during a typically unshowy demonstration of his affection while I was in full hysteric mode.

It was April 1994, and Jason and I had been dating since the previous fall. Alone in my dorm room at 2:00 a.m. one night, I felt unimaginable pain, as if a boogeyman beneath my bed were pushing up through it with a long, hot knife. Color me male, but I was convinced I was dying—that thought filled my head and sent me stumbling to my desk, searching for the phone to call 911.

While I waited for the ambulance that I had just ordered like a pizza, I felt compelled to write a note to my boyfriend. It was telling that after less than a year of dating my gut instinct was explicit. The note contained only the name Jason Greenwood, his phone number, and the words "I LOVE YOU." In retrospect, I can see how melodramatic I was being, not to mention how morbid it would have been for a paramedic to hand Jason a note found in the bathrobe pocket of my corpse. But, hey, I was dying, right? Who had time for sanity?

Turns out, I didn't need the note: I was going to live, albeit without my ruptured bile duct and my swollen-to-bursting gallbladder. Lying on a gurney, anaesthetized, in an operating room queue, I was signing forms: I will not sue for this; I will not cry foul at that; I will not hold the hospital responsible for damage to my teeth. *My teeth?* I laughed, thinking that if they hit my teeth on the way to my gallbladder, someone would have to be very badly lost.

I woke hours later to a series of indignities: the night nurse missing a vein; the first drip of Demerol making me puke; and every nurse within miles refusing my requests for water. When daylight filled the room, time dragged. Pain made me grumpy and my thoughts turned to Jason with less than charity. *Why hadn't he come to see me yet? What kind of boyfriend would make me wait whole hours for a visit? Maybe my sudden illness had scared him off—maybe he was afraid I was a bad health risk. Damn him! Didn't he know that when I wrote what I thought were my last words in the world, they were to him?*

Meanwhile, pragmatic as ever, knowing that I had not died and was in no peril of expiration, Jason had gone to his morning classes before coming to see me. He couldn't have imagined, when he stepped through the door, what sour air he was walking into. What I meant to say was "I'm so glad you're here." Or "I love you." What came out—surely it wasn't me talking—was whiny, shrill. "Why didn't you come sooner?" I railed on. "They're so mean to me. I can't have any water and they won't change my medicine and the middle-of-the-night nurse hates me!"

"Shhh," he soothed—did I detect a note of amusement? I refused to be patronized! So I grabbed my IV stand and hobbled to the bathroom, turning my back on the one visitor I had wanted, just moments after he arrived.

In the bathroom I tried to compose myself. But when I turned to face the mirror, I began to wail. "My teeth!" There was a puzzled pause before Jason knocked at the door and asked me to repeat myself.

I let him in to see. I was already insecure about an existing paper-thin gap between my front teeth; now a breathing apparatus used in surgery had widened the gap to what I saw as a yawning chasm. We both looked at my reflection in the mirror: sweat-matted hair pasted to my scalp, face splotchy and mottled, and this new grand canyon. Lovely. I was sure Jason would flee, repulsed.

He didn't. Instead, he led me back to the bed and found a wordless way to assure me that everything would be okay. Having sized up the situation and knowing the only cure was rest, he climbed onto the bed next to me, let me settle my damp head on his chest, and placed one arm under my neck. "You just go back to sleep," he said. I could hear his heartbeat as I closed my eyes, and I remember thinking to myself, I could marry this guy.

Indeed, I would, once I got inside the church. I had to ring the doorbell to get into my own wedding, but there I was, minutes to spare, sliding a bit on the slick floor and skidding directly into the path of my pacing honey. Our photographers caught the next moment: Jason's hands rest on my chest as I gaze up into his eyes; his lips are parted as if in laughter. We used this image—so very romance novel!—on our thank-you notes and wedding announcements, but the truth of the matter is this: I am telling him to breathe, and he is not laughing but saying, "I think I'm going to vomit."

Just about that moment, the music began to play. We had to get down the aisle, and by the pace of the sonata we were hearing through the chapel doors we didn't have much time. We joined hands and prepared to embark on our future. Would civilization collapse if we took those steps? Would happily married heterosexual couples suddenly feel awash in discontent? Would God smite the church with lightning?

I can't answer the first two questions, but I'm pretty sure no smiting took place. The next few hours were rich with everything we imagined a wedding would entail and also a few things we had not, from the friend of mine listening to a football game on a not-entirely-discreet earpiece during the service, to my mortifying-beyond-goyim pronunciation of "mazel tov" when we stepped on a glass as a nod to Jewish relatives. The good news, though, was that I never again lost sight of my pants and Jason kept his breakfast down.

Afterwards, as guests hugged their way through our receiving line, we had an encounter that became one of the highlights of the day. There was Grampa Greenwood, cowboy hat in hand, his white hair exposed and his eyes full of tears. I was so startled at the sight I blurted out, "You said a cowboy couldn't take his hat off." Voice thick, Grampa replied, "A cowboy can . . . but only for the most special occasions."

He wasn't the only grandparent to shed surprise tears. I found out later that when my grandmother had heard what I said about not being able to see my own family at my wedding, she had cried all day. I will never know what exactly her tears involved—hurt? shame? wounded pride?—for she didn't call me to say.

But I do know this. Exactly one week later, a package arrived at our Somerville apartment. In it, a set of Renee's towels, proof positive that I was married.

It was a gift that made *me* cry. And isn't that what weddings are all about?

2

Where Husbands Come From

No marriage starts at the altar. Despite the fact that the dj at my wedding decided it would be sweet to play the Carpenters' ballad "We've Only Just Begun," it simply isn't true. You can't start up the aisle until you've gotten to hello and, from there, rounded a few bases, endured a few fights, and found something worth defying our country's divorce statistics for. Considering all the things that can go wrong along the way—say, unreturned affection, a wandering eye, family disapproval—it's a wonder that anyone ever makes it to the church in the first place.

In the movies, the construct of Love at First Sight takes the worry out of that process. The first time the hero and heroine spot each other, a slow motion shot and a special musical cue heighten the moment. No matter what follows, the audience has been clearly instructed as to the outcome: these two are made for each other. But how do you replicate that in real life? How can you tell if you've found The One when time doesn't slow down and no touching soundtrack plays in your head?

The first time I laid eyes on the guy I would marry, I saw a cute young bohemian in a Guatemalan vest and cloth bracelets, who was edging his way through a restless crowd into my line of sight. No, we were not in a dance club; we were on the Boston Common ballfield, which had been filled with folding tables and banners for the Emerson College fall orientation fair. I was working the fair as president of the awkwardly named EAGLE: the Emerson Alliance of Gays, Lesbians, and Everyone.

It was my job to sit at the EAGLE table looking gay and approachable, so that prospective members would stop by and sign up for our meetings. As a graduate student, I was something of an anomaly in EAGLE, the membership of which was 90 percent undergrad, as evidenced by the cherubic faces of baby dykes and queer bois swarming the table in search of free buttons and vulgar bumper stickers. So when Jason, all of twenty-four, stepped forward, it was a relief to me to see what I considered an actual grown-up. And one who was easy on the eyes to boot.

Dark blonde hair fell across his forehead and parted to reveal bright blue eyes. His smile made a soft V in his beard, which—combined with the hair—gave him a Jesus-gone-indie-rock edge. He seemed comfortable with his body, a slender frame with a long torso, and he looked like a guy who could dance. But there was something else, a hint of playfulness mixed with guardedness, that made him very appealing. I began to worry about whether I looked all right in my Queer

Nation attire: a black beret pulled down in the back, a suit jacket over a T-shirt, and several of those metal-object-on-leather-string pendants so popular at the time. I tried to sit up and look less, well, short and overweight.

Thinking that I had to get to know this guy, I pushed my clipboard at him and asked him to write down his name and number, so "the group" could contact him if needed. I didn't actually say much; I was so concerned with appearing nonchalant and cool. Giving him a little smile that I hoped would be read as "thanks" without revealing that I was thinking "god, you're cute," I took back the clipboard and, once he stepped away, put a star next to his name so I would be sure to remember it when I saw him next. I suppose it wasn't so much love at first sight as lust with a dollop of intrigue. But that's my version.

His version is this: having finally gotten close enough to the table to introduce himself to the only other gay guy his age, he was merely asked his name and told to sign a sheet. I did not make much of a visual impression. Though I am Cuban-American, my father's family's roots go back to Spain, so my light skin and brown eyes don't read as particularly exotic. And it's not like I had dazzled him with conversation. Big whoop.

"Well, *he's* not very friendly," thought the man who had no idea he was being checked out. Keen to slights, having lived through the classic "sucks-to-be-gay" high school experience, Jason interpreted my scheming silence as a cold shoulder. "Whatever," he thought, moving away from the booth. "If he's gonna give people attitude, he might wanna rethink that beret."

Ah, romance.

Fortunately for us both, I am a dogged pursuer of things I want. And somehow I knew right away that I wanted Jason. A week later, when EAGLE had its first meeting, I was thrilled when he arrived—except that he was accompanied by his roommate, also a gay grad student, which posed a slight social dilemma. I had previously met the roommate, twice no less, but despite the fact that he was prone to shrieks and dramatic hand gestures and referred to himself as "the Queen" of his old school, he'd made so little an impression on me that I had forgotten his name. Having to be reminded who he was made it a smidge awkward when I greeted Jason by name, seemingly off the top of my head, trying desperately to sound casual. Jason took mental note of my specifically honed memory and, in that moment, realized how badly he'd misjudged our first encounter. That, as it turns out, was the last time that he misread me; from here on out, he would always be two or three steps ahead of me, and I, poor bastard, wouldn't have a clue.

Three days later, having waited as long as I could, I called him up at home. Why else keep a member directory, right? Ostensibly, I wanted his advice on how to lure more grad students to the group. There was a pause, which I took to be him mulling over the question, but which in fact was him thinking how nakedly thin was this ploy of mine, and wondering whether or not he should call me on it. Finally, he answered, "I really don't have any ideas on that, sorry," and then forged ahead. "So when can we meet for coffee?"

Clearly, he was better at this sort of thing than I was. My dating life to this point had not been especially, let's say, *comprehensive*. Perhaps as a holdover from my fundamentalist youth, I hadn't exactly walked on the wild side. My first date with a man—a handsome Irish photographer named Bob, who wasn't thrilled to learn that he was my first date—had occurred only eighteen months before. After that, I'd mostly had romantic missteps, not romances: a gold digger who moved on as soon as he discovered I was gold-free; a Polish kid who rubbed my head in an elevator, giggled a lot before kissing me, and never called again; the dancer who could read my mind—no, really—but was busy considering celibacy; the Cuban tenor who wanted to make out under the covers, as long as he could keep his clothes on; and the bookstore clerk who showed up for a date in full drag—and full beard. In truth, I'd only had one actual boyfriend, whom I'll call Trey: a bisexual dreamer-schemer who could talk a person into and out of anything; he was sure to either end up in the Senate (his goal) or selling real estate (my prediction). I found him sexy in his star-spangled briefs, and I loved the way he championed the liberating power of sex—except for when he was repulsed by it, a dichotomy that necessarily doomed our relationship.

That sums up my entire pre-Jason romantic life. Sometimes, when I read the literature of homophobes and see that we homos allegedly have hundreds of partners, it occurs to me that I may have let my people down by being so chaste, and let myself down by missing out on the hedonistic youth that everyone would assume I had anyway. Compared to my straight friends—like my grad school buddy Ben, who more than once had three girlfriends at the same party—my romantic life had been as uncomplicated and physically virtuous as that of a Promise Keeper.

Jason, on the other hand, while not having quite whittled down his bedpost to sawdust with notches, was nonetheless having a sex life more typical of the people in our generation, gay and straight alike. I would eventually hear stories of the summers he was the Cute Waiter Boy in a New Hampshire inn, including the time a Manhattan performance artist turned to Jason for some local color. And then there were his college years in sexed-up Montreal, which included the standard university blend of one-night stands and friends with benefits. But, over time, he also had a series of real boyfriends: the volatile pastor, the conflicted businessman, the hunky Quebecois sweetheart, the cute geek with a great nose, the secret Janet Jackson impersonator. Some of these relationships even lasted long enough for family members to meet and like the men.

In other words, Jason had already had the kind of life experience you'd expect for a sophisticated college grad; what he didn't have was time for coy pretense from a novice dater. Instead, he got the real reason for my call out on the table and I had no choice but to step up. We made a date for a few nights later.

Actually, we didn't make a "date"—we made a plan. We couldn't make a date because Jason was still dating someone, albeit long distance. Actually, Jason had declared that they were *not* dating anymore, but he'd been informed that "one person can't end a relationship—*both* have to say it's over." Having just been told that he had no power over breaking up with one guy, he could at least control whether or not he was dating a second guy now.

It certainly *felt* like a date. We ate an early dinner at Moka, a Back Bay café in Boston which had a quasi-California theme and cheap prices. I remember almost nothing about the conversation except that it flowed easily and flowed on and on . . . and then on some more. Our waiter, a snippy little queen who was made less warm by the fact that he was living off the kind of tips you make serving tortillas to grad students, removed our plates at the two-hour mark. Our dirty napkins and silver were next to go. Half an hour later, even our water glasses disappeared. Three hours into our evening, we took the hint.

It was dark when we stepped outside. By this time, I was determined that our nondate should not end and decided perhaps I could heighten things with a more romantic atmosphere. I led Jason to the sunken fountain in Copley Square: by day a skateboarders' hangout, the fountain was lovely by night, with granite steps cut into a green lawn and leading down to a basin where bright lights illuminated the rising-and-falling jets of water from below. I motioned for Jason to sit on the steps of the fountain and then joined him, leaning back with my elbows on the grass. It was a perfect night, with a deep blue sky and the city humming around us—a romantic's dream.

Except for the rat. Few things are less lovely than a rodent the size of your thigh scurrying by, and, just like that, my cinematic fantasy by the fountain evaporated.

Instead, we strolled along Newbury Street, Boston's high-end shopping destination. Newbury Street is a funny place—at one end, a tight-skinned matron can buy herself a clutch purse that costs more than the gross national product of a small island nation; seven blocks later, it's all about combat boots and used CDs. You can imagine which end we were headed for, engaging as we went in the kind of wistful scorn so common to half-broke grad students: mocking the pretentious crowd at Armani Café while wishing we had their shoes.

Once safely ensconced in a corner booth at Trident Café, a book-lover's paradise—and crossing the four-hour mark in our conversation—I found myself half listening to the story Jason was telling, about how his stepmother liked to joke that he drove her into therapy, and half just contemplating him from different mental angles. Personality? He was comfortable enough with himself to carry around a retro Scooby-Doo lunchbox. Brains? He was working on a Master of Science degree in speech therapy. Character? He planned to work with developmentally delayed kids for the rest of his life, god love him. Appearance? His hair fell across his blue eyes, which struck me as just about the sexiest thing ever. Taken together, that meant he was playful, smart, noble, *and* cute. I was hooked.

I spent the rest of the evening telegraphing my interest. Gee, I asked innocently, did I mention that my first serious crush was on *another* Jason? When swapping stories of cute guys—something we gay men are allowed to do—I mentioned a college hottie who was just covered in fur, a point I made while looking at Jason's hairy forearms. A guy can only pander or be pandered to for so long, and eventually, after seven hours and three locations, we wrapped up the best non-date I'd ever been on.

By our second unofficial date, a week later, we were already discussing children. Jason made it clear that he would never seriously date someone who did not want kids. I, of course, made my love of children abundantly plain: hadn't I worked at summer camp for nine years, not to mention been an aide at a grade school, taught at three high schools, worked with troubled boys, and run an urban youth program? This was all true, but it was also a comparative sales job, for I knew that Jason's previous boyfriend had never wanted children. Poor guy simply hadn't realized who he was dealing with in Jason.

Of course, neither did I. Soon enough I would learn that my new crush was the captain of mixed signals. A month into our undefined relationship, we drove to Mount Wachusett, a geographical hiccup in central Massachusetts, to ride the gondola together in peak leaf season—but then, though he sat with his knee touching mine, he didn't try to hold my hand. I didn't dare take his hand, because, technically, he was off limits with that whole distant not-yet-ex boyfriend, so I waited in vain for his move. A week or two later, when we dressed as Jesus and Buddha for Halloween, he suggested a photo of the two deities in bed together—but didn't ask me to sleep over.

One night as we drove home from an excursion together, he told me that I was handsome—but then pulled out photos of the old boyfriend and asked me if I thought he was making a mistake by ending things. Worse, whenever I would hint that maybe we should crank things up a notch, Jason would reply with some variant of "I'm not ready to date again—I should probably be on my own for a while, blah blah yadda yadda blah blah—so what are we doing Saturday night?"

By this point, he and I were spending so much time together that my clever friend Ricia coined a nickname for Jason: The Guy You're Not Seeing. As a former fundamentalist Cuban-American, my multiple cultures have together yielded a person who is faithful, passionate, and emotionally dramatic— in other words, the kind of guy who can be made insane by this nondating business. I simply couldn't look at other guys seriously while thinking of Jason so much, and I couldn't stop thinking of him as long as there was any chance it would work out. But every time I considered getting off the Jason carousel, he would do something that kept me on board.

A prime example is the November afternoon that he unexpectedly brought me a loaf of homemade banana bread in a paper bag, upon which he had listed, in very small letters, the following ingredients: bananas, sugar, butter, eggs, flour, baking soda, love, and walnuts. Pardon me, but one should never, ever use the word *love,* even jokingly, with a romantic like me, unless the intent is to wildly raise the stakes. This gift both touched me and made we wonder whether I needed to back off for my own emotional safety.

I was already keyed up because we were supposed to go to a Tuck & Patti jazz concert the next night. In two months of nondating, we had listened to this duo's tapes on so many long drives together that their songs had come to represent our relationship—whatever the hell it was. I wasn't sure how I would feel during the concert, when the music would be live but our romance still only imagined. By the afternoon of the concert, I was so wound up that a bizarre thing happened: my throat began to close up.

I ended up in the emergency room, where a resident sat puzzled, flipping through a book of medical symptoms before imploring me to swallow a milkshake of muscle relaxant—no small task since my throat was swollen shut. I wanted to argue, but it seemed easier to find a way to inhale the horrible liquid through a plastic straw, reproaching the resident with my eyes, as he looked on with the desperate expression of a man completely without other suggestions. Fortunately for my pending date and the resident's nerves, it worked. Once I could breathe normally again, he sent me on my way, chalking the matter up to stress. Clearly, something had to change.

When I met Jason on the sidewalk in front of the Berklee Performance Center and explained what had happened, he didn't venture a guess as to why, but he had a knowing look on his face. Later in the darkened balcony, as Patti sang, "Sometimes it amazes me, how strong the power of love can be," Jason found my hand with his own and squeezed it. He kept his eyes ahead, never looking at me, and when the song ended he let go. He did not speak of this on the way back to campus, and when we arrived in front of my dorm he said he couldn't come up because he had to work the next morning. I was so baffled I wanted to cry. It was lightly snowing when, quietly, he kissed my head. Not my lips or cheek—that would have been too direct—just the top of my head. And I, the one who craved this for so long? I bolted away like a cow that has backed into an electric fence, then fled into the building.

The next day I called Jason up to tell him that he was killing me. Yes, I loved our time together, and yes, I thought of him the rest of the time. But I hated pursuing him like some groupie or stalker, especially in the face of his constant disavowals. If things weren't really going anywhere with us, he needed to tell me straight out and not just hypothetically, because I simply did not have the constitution to keep this up. Trying to sound calm, I asked, "Is that what you need—for me to let this go?" When he didn't answer, I told him I would understand if the answer was yes, but that I also had to stop devoting so much time to him. And then, because I couldn't help myself, I added, "If I'm getting this all wrong and you really don't want me to give up, then you need to hold out a light." Otherwise, I said, I was gone.

Give an ultimatum to a man who badly wants control of a situation, and this is what you get: evasion. His whole answer was, "Can we talk about this tomorrow?" Unbelievable. He must have known how hard it was for me ask a question like this once, and, damn the banana-bread-wielding bastard, he was going to make me ask twice.

That night, crying to an endless loop of Tuck & Patti on my Walkman, I took a train west to my old college town to get consolation from my friends Neal, Amy, and Ingrid. Sitting in the Denny's where we'd always done our late-night cramming as undergrads, I received conflicting advice: Neal said, "Why let him decide? You should do whatever you need"; Ingrid, furious, said, "Dump the jerk"; and Amy, who is always right about everything, asked, "Isn't it a little early to mourn the loss of someone who might still say he's interested?" I couldn't know, sitting there with French fries in one hand and Kleenex in the other, that someday Neal would drive me to get my wedding pants while Jason paced at the church; Amy would be lighting our unity candle; and, seeing as we didn't need a legal officiant, Ingrid would perform the wedding service. I knew only that they were there for me that night, reminding me of my value with or without The Guy I Wasn't Seeing.

Thus fortified, I sat in my dorm room the next day waiting for Jason's call with tissues in hand. Bracing myself, I vowed this time to let him do the talking. And then he blew me away. "Of *course* I'm interested," he said. "I love all that you've done for me." He had deeply enjoyed being pursued, had kept his friends abreast of my efforts, but had not wanted to reveal this to me too soon. He meant it when he said, "Don't give up on me." Barring the fact that we officially became a couple while not even in the same room, I was a happy man.

Typically, at this point, I'd have a boyfriend. But that would be too easy. Having revealed his interest, Jason demurred at applying labels so soon. To him, the term "boyfriend" seemed so much more, well, *something* than "dating." So that was that—even once we were sleeping together, once I had spent the holidays with his family, even once the hometown boyfriend had been made aware of his replacement—Jason was The Guy I Was Seeing, but no more. This remained true for several months, until one sleepover when I was curled up next to him in bed and a friend called him from Canada. At some point in their chat, I made a comment in the background, and the friend asked Jason who else was there. "Oh him?" he replied without thinking. "That's my boyfriend, Dave." I sat bolt upright: he *so* could not start using the term without telling me. Or, well, yes, he could and he had. When he got off the phone he gave a sheepish smile and shrugged. "It was the easiest way to say it." Well, *duh*.

Over the following months, we became more officially a couple in a number of ways: supporting each other through things like illness and the stress of a job search; cohabitating as I moved into the basement apartment he already shared with a roommate; and spending two weeks of vacation housesitting in the Bay Area, together nearly 'round the clock without either of us threatening murder. It was an August night, at the end of that quasi vacation, when we realized we had both started talking about our future in unison—where "we" wanted to live and where "we" could both find jobs. When we acknowledged this change of pronoun out loud, after nearly a year together, the possibility of a wedding also came up. In 1994, of course, a wedding was as good as it got—legal marriage was for couples with only one Y chromosome in the mix.

I'm a romantic, so that conversation should have delighted me. But, for very good reason, I had terrifying visions of Jason proposing as an aside during a phone call—"Oh him? That's the guy I'm asking to marry me." I decided to preempt that outcome by planning to propose myself just two weeks later on the September day we moved into our first apartment alone together.

After we moved in the last box, we sat on the floor amid our unpacked things to eat Chinese take-out while listening to—no surprise here—Tuck & Patti. I handed Jason a home-made calendar recounting our first year together, marked with each important nondate, surprise throat-closing, and change of status from friend to boyfriend. I timed things so that just as Tuck & Patti were starting the song they were singing when Jason first held my hand, he'd get to the last page of the calendar, September 2004.

That page was blank except for two words: *Dave proposes.*

I looked at Jason, and his eyes were bright. He made a little "oh" sound and leaned in toward me. I'd like to say that Jason was surprised by my proposal, but he wasn't. The upside for him of always being one step ahead of me was that he had control over his response. And this time, thank god, I didn't have to ask twice.

3

~

Two Hearts Beat as Two

WE CELEBRATED VALENTINE'S DAY, 1995, OUR FIRST AS newlyweds, in the manner that would come to define the holiday for us: we ate Chinese. *With friends.* That's right, no rendezvous in a dimly lit bistro, no two-man hot tub surrounded by candles. It was a group outing for moo shu pork and General Gau's chicken, and everyone escaped unscathed. Which is more than can be said of the previous Valentine's Day.

The year before, still getting to know each other as a couple, I made a serious miscalculation about my honey's temperament. He knew I had made reservations at a nice Chinese restaurant but didn't know what else I had up my sleeve until I told him to pack an overnight bag. He was reluctant, not out of modesty, but out of a desire not to relinquish control of his evening. I cajoled him into complying (cajoling was a dominant trait in those early months) and off we went.

Dinner was excellent; typical of us, we ordered way more food than two people should consciably have to themselves and then ate off each other's plates unabashedly. The problem was my plan for dessert: I had booked us a room at a Victorian inn just down the street from the restaurant, intending a night of old school romance. A candlelit parlor, a huge four-poster bed—it was to be simply swoon-inducing. Unless, of course, you are Jason, and it appears that you have been told what to do—which, I admit, he had. In that case, it looked like a musty old hotel for which money has been spent only to require him to sleep in a strange bed for the night.

Let us close this story with a simple statement: only sleep took place.

It was one of my first introductions to the truth about relationships, even good ones. All the gooey crap you hear about "two hearts beating as one" is just that: gooey crap. Two hearts beat quite independently, thank you, and every pair of lovers comes with two ways to do and see everything. In the first years, then, life as a couple is all about discovering just how many things you can approach differently without actually killing each other. It is remarkable how many firm opinions one can hold on domestic matters, regardless how mundane, from laundry to housekeeping. Jason folds his underwear, which stunned me; I make "sock balls" with my dirty socks, which appalled him. I thought it was much more sanitary to place glasses with their rims down, though his instinct was rims up.

Consider the minor detail of how a roll of toilet paper hangs on the bar. Jason comes from "paper over" country, so that the next sheet dangles exposed and, in his logic, is easier to reach. My people were devout "paper under" people, so the loose end is discreetly against the wall, not flapping flagrantly about. Jason thought I was insane the first time I changed the roll of paper. What moron would make the next sheet harder to reach? I was aghast: who wants to leave the roll exposed, risking sudden unspooling? This debate, though short-lasting, involved scorn applied not just to each other but to each other's families, who received the blame for such habits existing in the first place. See how quickly a tiny topic can flare up into an Identity Issue? It wouldn't surprise me at all if the high divorce rate in our country has to do with the fact that no one is talking to young couples about toilet paper.

A more pressing need, for me, I suppose, would have been a warning about groceries. Maybe this isn't an issue for every couple, especially if only one party always does the shopping, but we were all into equity, and so we did our shopping together. I was entirely unprepared for the result.

You see, I grew up on welfare. Food stamps kind of kill the whole supermarket experience, if you ask me, and even though I am now beyond my government cheese days, I still approach a grocery store like the smart bomb of shoppers— hitting my target and nothing else. My basic approach has three parts: go with a list in hand; figure out the shortest route between the listed items and *only* those items; leave as quickly as possible. I'd prefer to limit each sortie to ten or fifteen minutes, unless we have a whole week's worth of groceries to buy, in which case I could (barely) stand twenty minutes.

My husband, on the other hand, comes from the Market-as-Museum school of thought, in which a person must not risk missing any of the collected treasures. No matter what the list in his hand includes, he is perfectly content to grab a big, empty cart at the door and head for the furthest aisle, where he will begin a dreamy stroll through the entire store. That's right, aisle by aisle, drifting from the front of store to the back and then the front again, he wouldn't dream of cutting corners and skipping a section. What if there was an unannounced sale on extra virgin olive oil? What if tortilla chips were half price? What if there was some gooey cheese the store didn't usually carry or a new flavor of Ben & Jerry's? Hurrying through was out of the question: with "slow and steady" as his motto, an hour could just fly by before Jason even approached a register.

I could have killed him. Or myself. I grew bored waiting for him to finish comparing the leanness of various brands of turkey burger. I would try to nudge him past the face cleansers with a plea that I had work to do at home. He would counter with the heart-tugging reminder that he loved supermarkets and it was unfair to make him give up a source of pleasure. And so it went, shopping trip after shopping trip. This led to a complete meltdown once in a Star Market, which is an absurd place for melodrama, surrounded as you are by melons and boxes of Captain Crunch. Fortunately, there was one thing that could save us from the trauma of shopping: having dinner together afterward with the bounty. If one thing has ever re-mained true of us, a good meal cures all ills.

While some of our newlywed tussles were over the practical matters, perhaps the biggest adjustment was admitting that we had very different emotional instincts as well. To explain, let me quote one definition of the Yiddish term *schmaltz*:

Schmaltz: (N) Effusive sentimentality.

And then let me add to that a little definition of my own:

Schmaltzball: (N) A person given to schmaltz.

I am a schmaltzball and, it is unlikely to surprise you to learn, Jason is not.

This should have been clear to me earlier, but—like any good romantic—I had been blinded by the novelty of new love. When we were dating, I mooned over him—bringing him flowers, writing him a song, all that kind of goo—while he remained ever practical. His first gift to me was a bar of soap, handed to me while driving. Despite the mixed messages in a gift of soap, I was touched because he had chosen it and, hell, it was a *present*.

The longer we were together, the more this dynamic became clear. One March, when winter had finally worn him down as it always did, I spent hours converting the bedroom into a spring fantasy; he came home to find an enormous homemade crepe paper sun, a construction paper tree in bloom, a rattan bird's nest with candy robin's eggs, real pussy willows, and freshly cut daffodils.

His next gift to me was a magazine subscription.

I didn't expect him to keep up with my displays of affection—who could, really?—but I wondered why he couldn't summon up even the occasional unabashedly romantic impulse. My longing for a Grand Display often left him paralyzed between a desire not to disappoint me and a reluctance to perform on command like a trained seal of love.

If we thought toilet paper preferences or grocery shopping styles could create tension, we had seen nothing yet. On our first non-housesitting trip together, we spent a week in Vermont's "Northeast Kingdom" (abandon all hope ye city folk who enter here), where our opposing romantic notions were thrown into high relief. We had set ourselves up for this I suppose, by planning a lakeside vacation on the border of Canada on the brink of September. The leaves were already changing, mocking us for thinking of this as a late-summer getaway; the crystal clear lake we had paid to be on was, by this time, too cold for more than the briefest bone-chilling swim.

In the first few days, the sun played peek-a-boo behind a few grey clouds and we donned sweaters for excursions to see the local sights. Unfortunately, each sight was an hour's drive apart from any other, with nothing but country between. Worse, some of the sights included a demolition derby and a wood-craft fair with objets d'art like a stunning rifle-shaped door hanging emblazoned with the words, "We don't call 911."

It was soon clear that two city dwellers might well run short of things that reflected their interests in this rural king-dom. But we told ourselves that we could at least fill the week with canoeing and hiking along woodland paths. Except that on the third day it began to rain. As it did on the fourth day. And the fifth. By day six, we had been in our two-room cabin for four days straight and the strain was beginning to show.

Before I explain what happened next, let me describe this haven of delight. The smaller room was the bedroom, whose two furnishings were a bed adorned with one of those nubbly blankets grandparents are so fond of and a painfully detailed plastic crucifix directly above the headboard. Now, I know that some fetishists find asphyxiation sexy, but a crucifix just strikes me as a pretty big buzzkill—which may well have been the point.

Just beyond Jesus' line of sight, the main room was a kitchen/dining-room/living-room combo with a half dozen windows, all providing a different view of the scenery: rain on the lake, rain on the deck, rain on the picnic table, and so on.

Otherwise, the room featured very little other than a TV with two working channels and four—count 'em, four—couches to watch those channels from.

Jason's way of dealing with the tension of this now obviously ruined vacation was to curl up, figuratively and literally. He chose a spot on one of the couches and disappeared into a book. He was ominously quiet, which is his way of saying "I'm pissed about something," and I wanted to somehow break the spell. As a romantic, I decided that the best approach was to show a united front: we didn't have to be *doing* anything—we just needed to be together. I grabbed my own book and snuggled up next to him, sure that we'd both feel better.

Jason stiffened. Despite knowing that he's a man who needs his space, I had taken the smallness of the cabin and rendered it even smaller, trapping him inside my "love me" bubble, when what he really wanted more than anything was room.

The cabin, impossibly, grew more quiet. He spoke as calmly as he could. "Of all the couches in this stupid cabin, you had to sit on this one?" And with that, he got up, put on a raincoat and went for a walk in the downpour.

When he came back, we did what couples are supposed to do: we apologized—me for crowding, him for fleeing—and acknowledged that the real issue was that this vacation sucked big time. Our disappointment wasn't with each other but with the fact that our one week off had gone swirling down the drainpipe. And so we did the right thing: we blew off the last day of our rental and packed up, heading south a couple of hours to Northampton, where there were restaurants, shops, and people other than ourselves to mock. We checked into an Econolodge and there, having let go of the imagined ideal of our vacation, we had the best night of the week. Let me close this story by saying: *more* than sleep took place.

That week set a good precedent for surviving every difference that raised its head in our relationship. Just freeing ourselves up from preconceptions of how anything is "supposed to be" allowed us to live with how things actually were. We discovered that difference could be just that: difference, not crisis.

Some things, as it turned out, didn't require solving: Jason still folds his undies; I still make sock balls. And other issues were solved relatively painlessly: I held my ground and won on the glasses, but he won on the toilet paper. Understandably, for a few topics, it required a smidge more effort to reach détente.

Resolving the grocery store matter involved my husband tricking me. He began bringing me to Wilson Farms, which is housed in a big faux barn, the food arrayed on rustic wooden pallets and in barrels, all bathed in mood lighting. It was like going to a theme park or the elaborate set of an opera about produce. Of course I loved it. Every October, Wilson Farms had fresh caramel apples, which I'm a sucker for, and then those were cleared away to make room for Thanksgiving pies, which themselves were replaced by gingerbread houses in December. Season by season, it was never the same market two visits in a row, and suddenly I found time to shop.

Once he had eased me into spending time on groceries, Jason got me into the groove of regular shopping as well by tag-teaming our Wilson Farms visits with a trip to the nearest supermarket. But he also knew better than to endlessly exploit my new willingness, so he began to stick more closely to a list himself. We got our market runs down to respectable half-hour excursions, and when he truly wanted to wallow in groceries, he went without me. A Golden Rule of Couples: "Do by yourself that which your sweetie doesn't want to do with you."

It took slightly longer for me to completely come around on what seemed like his unromantic nature. First, I tried baiting him—sounding like my grandmother as I sighed, "It sure would be nice sometimes to come home and find a surprise waiting for me"—and then I went the wait-nobly-in-silence route, hoping my patience and long suffering would somehow inspire spontaneous emotional combustion on his part. No dice.

But eventually I learned to spot the underlying romance in more mundane actions: the way he is sure to add a caramel apple to the Wilson Farms grocery list each October; his swearing outrage at anyone who deals me the slightest ill treatment; his willingness to read the first knobby draft of every new play or column I write. And the way a snowstorm can make him happy, because it means we'll spend the day making cookies and watching videos together.

Even so, I'm still a schmaltzball. The first time a florist delivery man ever handed me a dozen long-stemmed roses from my husband, I got all teary because the gesture was so unlike the eternal pragmatist I had come to know. When Jason got home that night, he gently explained that the roses were really just a by-product of his making a donation to NPR. I had to laugh: he wasn't a new man—he was the one I'd loved all along.

And that's the man with whom I look forward to celebrating Valentine's Day year after year in Chinese restaurants. Over time, the tradition has gotten even further removed from the soft lens image of a Hollywood movie. It might well involve the kind of place that has a lagoon in the middle of the dining room, and is less likely to involve candles than drinks that are set aflame. Surrounded by friends, caught up in waves of laughter, and deeply content, I am sure to shoot my sweetie a dreamy isn't-life-grand look and then, because gooey crap is gooey crap, he'll roll his eyes at me in response—not a bad tradition, if you ask me.

More Than
Meets the "I Do"

4

A Pansy by Any Other Name?

JASON AND I CERTAINLY FELT MARRIED. IF YOU LOVE someone enough to pick up the clutter trail streaming in his wake for years, you must be pretty damn domesticated. We used the term "husband" for each other as if it was the most natural thing in the world—despite the fact that in 1996 civil unions and legal marriage were both still only dreamed notions, four and eight years away respectively. But no matter how obvious we thought our relationship appeared, once we stepped out of our own apartment, there was a whole big world out there to misunderstand us.

A couple doesn't have to be composed of two grooms without a bride to discover that people love to judge other people's relationships and that there's really no way to control what people do or don't respect. In my family alone, Grammy had a bone to pick with just about every marriage ever. Consider her three sons: one married a woman twice his age; another married his second wife after leaving the mother of his eight children; and a third married a lovely girl that Grammy truly liked, but who had the misfortune of being Catholic, a sticking point because Grammy believed that the Pope was the Anti-Christ. Her daughters did no better: her youngest went off and married a Cuban immigrant; and her eldest, twice widowed, was in her sixties when she married for a third time—prompting Grammy's weary complaint, "She's just gonna bury herself another one."

Even before I married a man, my own generation was working Grammy's nerves with our trips down the aisle. When my brother married his third wife before age thirty, Grammy rolled her eyes at the news and bit the inside of her cheek to keep silent, before blurting out, "Well, I already met two; I'm not about to meet a third." One cousin married a black man (big news in rural Maine in those days), which unintentionally topped her sister, who had previously walked down the aisle with her first child visibly stretching the empress waist of her wedding gown. That Grammy came to approve of each of those marriages, two of which have lasted to this day, does not change the fact that she raised her eyebrows at first for all three.

I'm sure plenty of marriages, unlike those in my family, do fit the mainstream American ideal: two people of opposite sex but otherwise of the same age, race, class, religion, and previous marital history, for whom neither the how nor the why of their relationship raises questions. But for the many millions of couples who don't meet that description, there is always that moment of hesitation in a new setting, the little hiccup of time when they must wonder just how the love they've chosen will be seen. As for Jason and me, the stakes were raised even more by the fact that we lacked the formal sanction of legal marriage, which would have at least provided others with a clear definition of whom and what they were rolling their eyes at.

Jason and I were reminded of the novelty of our union in countless ways, most often in professional settings. As a preschool speech therapist, pretty much everywhere Jason worked he was the only guy on staff and, typically, also the first out gay person. This put him in the unusual position of being a white male who was the diversity hire. Add to that his same-sex marriage and he was like some exotic species that had wandered out of its ecosystem. Of course, it wasn't exotic to him; he listed me as his spouse on job applications and always wore a wedding ring, so he figured that things were perfectly clear. His employers weren't always sure.

One evening, we were sitting at home when Jason received a call in which he was offered a job working with infants and toddlers. His new boss, an inspiring blend of professional savvy and interpersonal warmth, told him she'd be having a team meeting the next day to discuss the imminent arrival of a man on their all-female team. She asked Jason whether there was anything else he hoped she'd bring up at that meeting. Nosy bastard that I am, I was using Jason's verbal responses to figure out what his new employer was saying, and I also knew his body language well enough to immediately intuit what she was asking. "I can't think of anything," he said, shrugging, even as I poked him in the arm trying to get his attention. (Why marry a man if you're not going to react when he's jabbing at you like a madman?) They ended their conversation, while I groaned that he had ignored what even I, not on the phone, knew the employer was asking.

"What is wrong with you?" he asked, swatting me away.

"Did you hear what she was asking you?" I snarked.

"She wanted to know if there was anything else, and I . . . "

"She wanted to know if she can tell them that you're a gay guy married to a man."

"She did?" He first looked dumbstruck and then, in his defense, wondered why she wouldn't have just said so. I assured him that this was a measure of her sensitivity to his privacy, but I pointed out that she also probably expected him to see through this and give her some direction. Goaded into calling her back, he said that it had "just occurred" to him that she might want to tell his new colleagues about his relationship. With permission granted, she admitted that yes, indeed, that was exactly what she had been fishing for.

It wasn't that she thought there would be a problem, but she felt it was only fair to get it all out on the table, in case anyone needed time to digest the information. Ever sensitive in her treatment of others, the new boss simply wanted to let the full picture sink in for Jason's coworkers-to-be. Fortunately, his colleagues immediately embraced him (and, by extension, us), and that year I was just another one of the staff husbands at their holiday party. But the need for a discussion in the first place explains in a nutshell what it meant to be gay and married before such an institution truly existed: even gay-positive people had to take in the information, and rewire their synapses to allow for a husband who didn't come with a wife.

Imagine, then, just how hard it must be for people for whom even the fact of gayness requires mental adjustment.

Jason and I went to the small town of South Lancaster, Massachusetts, for Alumni Weekend at Atlantic Union College, the Seventh-day Adventist school I had attended as an undergrad. Young Alumni—those of us under thirty—had been invited back for a free pizza party, and the event seemed like a fun and nonreligious way to see old classmates, most of whom were still devout. Adventists not being fire-breathing fundamentalists, no one was going to chase me away from the event for showing up with Jason, but our appearance did give a few people pause. When one former classmate asked who my friend was, he had his hand extended before he heard my answer; when I said "my husband," his hand went limp. (Well, limper than usual; he never did have a strong grip.) But my freshman year roommate's response was most telling of all.

Also named Dave—as three out of four of us in our dormitory suite were—he'd left the school after one term and had never returned. I hadn't seen Dave in years, but there he was with his pretty new wife. When I introduced Jason as my new husband, he smiled and shook Jason's hand with no qualms at all. But as soon as Jason was distracted by a friend of ours, Dave took me aside and asked in a voice strained with dismay, "How did you get stuck being the wife?" I blanked—what was he talking about it? He saw my confusion and asked again, *sotto voce,* "Why does *he* get to be the husband?" When I finally caught up with his meaning, I laughed and explained that there was no wife at all, just us two husbands. I didn't press Dave on the gender issues involved in his visceral reaction to the idea of me being the wife; I figured we were being educational enough for one day.

Typically, of course, Jason and I weren't spending a lot of time in places where people still read the story of Sodom and

Gomorrah as having a happy ending. But sometimes, even in the places we most expected to pass unnoticed, we found that our union drew attention. This was true in Ogunquit, a beach town in Maine that is famously a gay destination. Having made a weekend trip to experience this queer-friendly town for ourselves, we were startled to find remnants of old cultural tensions simmering in the open. Few businesses at that time flew rainbow gay pride flags, and even the gay bars were discreetly marked. Once inside the gay piano bar or a gay inn, gay couples were seen in abundance. But on the streets, there was a strange cloaked feel. We didn't see same-sex couples holding hands like the straight couples; for that matter, it almost seemed as if the gay people were somehow getting from one gay hotspot to the next without using the streets.

We had come from the beach and were strolling up the main drag in search of ice cream. Both dressed in shorts and the square-cut retro shirts that had just come back into fashion, and sporting short haircuts, we looked pretty interchangeable with millions of guys our age in the mid-1990s. What made us look really gay, I suppose, was the fact that we were holding hands. I loved being able to hold Jason's hand in public—I'm that kind of guy, after all. There were too many places we didn't feel safe doing such a thing, but that's half the fun of going to a gay resort town: you can be sweet on your honey without a qualm. Unless, of course, straight couples start glaring at you for breaking the unspoken rule in which you were supposed to keep this sort of behavior indoors. It was surreal. Parents actually pulled their kids closer as we approached the ice cream shop. It was noticeably quieter around us than one would expect in the middle of a summer's day ice cream line. Here we were, in a town that derives substantial revenue from gay business, and we felt not just watched but disapproved of.

I should say here that we have not heard any similar tales from Ogunquit recently; for all we know, our experience was unusual even ten years ago. But that it did happen at all took us completely by surprise, and it sucked the sunlight out of the afternoon. We ordered our ice cream and then stepped away from the window, knowing we'd have to retrace our steps past the disapproving crowd. Holding our cones, we had a natural excuse for not holding hands anymore. But I wasn't going to give in that easily. To hold a cone takes only one hand; with the other, I took Jason's hand in mine as we began the walk back to the car. I still can't imagine what those people expected to see when they headed out for their afternoon in gay Ogunquit, but this is what they got: a man and his husband, strolling hand in hand like lovers do, unwilling to pretend otherwise.

I had a larger crowd to contend with when I took a part-time gig at a school outside of Boston. Massachusetts is not, as many would have it, a completely unchecked liberal bastion. This is evidenced by four successive Republican governors. But Jason and I lived on the left bank of the Charles River, which is to say the most liberal neck of the woods imaginable, so it was easy for us to forget that the notion of universal liberality was just a myth. My very brief career at a high school two trains and a bus ride south of the city set me straight in this regard.

I had agreed to a half-time teaching position at the high school in order to supplement the anemic income I made as an adjunct professor. I'd enjoyed everyone I had met on the staff, but the teacher prep days before the first class revealed that I had my work cut out for me: despite having just received many thousands of dollars in state funding, the school could not provide textbooks for some of my classes, or, for that matter, even enough seats. I myself would have no desk and would be expected to carry all my materials for the day from class to class, but I could hardly complain considering that I would have seatless, book-free students. While this state of affairs made me question the school's educational values, I soon discovered what it did value: the sanctity of marriage.

I found this out on the last day before classes began. All the teachers and staff had assembled in the auditorium, where the principal introduced the new hires. He asked us each to stand at the front, and to tell our names, where we lived and, oddly, whom we lived with. By this, he meant our marital status and whether we had children. The teacher immediately preceding me announced that she and her fiancé lived in a nearby town. A low murmur swept the room, the meaning of which was something like "the brazen hussy isn't just living in sin but announcing it!"

I hadn't fully processed the crowd's response to that announcement because it was already my turn; I cheerfully introduced myself and said I lived with my husband in Somerville. There was an audible gasp, and then it was very, very quiet. I took the silence to merely reflect the slow-to-warm nature of New Englanders, and, since they did applaud mildly when I sat down, I wasn't too deeply concerned. But as soon as the assembly was over, I learned how seismic my announcement had been. "That was so brave of you," whispered a dark-haired woman I had never met, patting my hand. "I have nothing against gays myself," crooned another, "but . . . " She shrugged and never finished the sentence. A young teacher who'd been there only a year or two took me aside at lunch to say, "It's probably no big deal, but you should know it's not that kind of school. Even the gay student group has a straight sponsor."

I wanted to say, "Oh, for god's sake—it's just a *word*, people." Except that, clearly, it wasn't. If the faculty could be shocked by a young woman who was sensibly living with her fiancé before legally binding herself to him, they'd naturally go apoplectic to think I had a husband. It became clear that some among the assembled crowd were sure that the brazen hussy and the man-marrying homo would be terrible moral influences on the students. It was no scandal to hold classes without chairs or books, but to hire sexually active teachers without marriage licenses? For shame!

I only taught there one day. For reasons unrelated to my marriage, the school decided to pay me 25 percent less than promised. As I found my pay cut even more shocking than my fellow teachers seemed to find the word *husband,* I decided to take a bus and two trains north and never look back.

Before that experience, I had always prided myself on not using such evasive language as "spouse"; like it or lump it, I was going to say "husband." But, in retrospect, I can't be too smug about my linguistic bravado, for it came from a place of ease: I'd been teaching in downtown Boston at Emerson College, lefty home of hipsters, swingers, and arty freaks. Until that day in the south shore high school, I'd been safely ensconced in a setting where it was a low-risk proposition to introduce myself as being married to a man. "At Emerson," one of my old students had boasted to me, "*everyone*'s gay for a night." That was a wild overstatement, to be sure, though not a bad reflection of the school's open attitudes toward sexuality.

But then, one year after my day teaching high school, I left Emerson to become a lecturer in English at Northeastern University. The new position offered admittedly crappy pay, and Jason wasn't allowed to share my medical insurance. But the job did come with retirement benefits, a renewable contract, and a title that looked nominally better on a resume than "desperate adjunct." Thrilled as I was at my incremental move up the career ladder, when I met my students—all 125 of them in five sections—I realized that I wasn't entirely prepared for the ethos of my new school.

Three of every four boys wore perfectly hand-tattered ballcaps; in similar numbers, the girls had their hair pulled back in ponytails or tied up in scrunchies. Their sweatshirts—and they were nearly all in sweatshirts—spoke of their affinity for athletic teams, Abercrombie & Fitch, and places to snowboard. These kids seemed sporty. *Butch*, even.

I had gotten so used to the Emerson kids that I had almost forgotten that other kinds of students existed. My classroom discussions at Emerson had been peppered with the references I knew they'd relate to: quotes from films, lines from Sondheim, and plenty of liberal blather. But here I was, facing row upon row of kids who I assumed preferred beer pong to Beckett, and I paused as I considered how to introduce myself. If "husband" had upset my fellow educators on the south shore, how would it go over among the working-class future linebackers of Northeastern? My guess: not well.

As a gay guy, my general reaction to groups of young men in sportswear has always been a slight flurry of panic. Granted, I had only once been threatened with death by a homophobic football player who slammed me up against a wall of metal hooks, but it's amazing how convincing such an event can be:

ever after, I was prone to all kinds of wild generalizations about jocks. Still, this was clearly *my* issue; nothing in the behavior of my new students even remotely indicated that I was headed for a tabloid headline: "Faggy Professor Whooped by Freshman Class."

As I looked over the room, I knew that saying that I had a husband would not make my students better writers, but, considering how endlessly and unthinkingly straight marriages are celebrated in our culture, my statement would be a part of the education I provided. (Yes, that sounds like I'm recruiting, but trust me: no student, gay or straight, ever signed up to be married in my class. Not once.) And so, recent past experience notwithstanding, I bit the bullet. "I'm David Valdes Greenwood, and I'm a writer living with my husband in Somerville," I announced, before going on to talk about my writing and teaching experience.

In the first class of the day, this merited no response at all. Nor in the second, third, or fourth. It was only in my last class that a guy wearing Northeastern's baseball team gear nudged and winked at the guy next to him as I spoke. But that was all—and he seemed thoroughly engaged for the rest of the day's session. Butch or not, they turned out to be wonderful kids, great to teach, and I enjoyed my time with them immensely. I even grew adept at sprinkling sports metaphors and booze analogies into my lectures. Defensively fearful of my students' stereotypes about gay people, I had preemptively given in to stereotypes about them instead. *Nice.*

The (non)reaction of my college students seemed a hopeful sign. I'd like to think it's because their generation has grown up seeing more of every kind of relationship—gay, interracial, intergenerational—and that this has given them a much broader vision of marriage than the one promoted by past generations. But it may also be that, at eighteen, they were still just young enough to remember the innocent years when "normal" was whatever they saw before them and exposure to prejudice had not yet distorted their sight.

Jason's kids were in those halcyon years. His preschool students never knew anything about his having a husband or even about his being gay, a concept beyond them. All they knew was that their teacher was a little different than most of their dads: he was a man who baked with them, sang them showtunes, and liked to play dress-up.

One day during circle time on the floor, Jason pulled out a box of hats. As he tried on the different hats, the children called out what he was supposed to be, instinctively matching image to association. Blue cap with a star? "Policeman!" they cried. Tall white toque? "A chef!" And when he donned a paper Burger King crown, the wise three year-olds chorused in one voice: "A *Queen!*" It wasn't as if he was wearing a ball gown or elbow gloves, but his kids were too young to be gender-purists. They looked at the person before them and went with the answer that (hilariously) was most true, even if inaccurate by dictionary standards.

I think, until the world teaches them otherwise, children simply see things as they are in a way that we grown-ups too often can't or won't. My own life is proof of this. The summer before first grade, I was kissing the neighbor boy when I first heard the term "pansy." When I asked Grammy what that meant, she washed my mouth out with soap before sighing with disdain, "It's what you call a man who loves a man like he's supposed to love a woman." She meant to make that sound abhorrent and awful, but instead, the whole idea instinctively made sense to me. Unfortunately for me, I said so out loud, which made her wash my mouth out with soap again and send me to bed without the salmon stew she'd made for supper.

Over the years, I would hear other terms—fag, homo, maricon—for these men she spoke of, but no matter what they were called, I was perfectly clear that the term applied to me. I was sure I was a pansy and that meant I would be marrying the neighbor boy. For, with the wisdom of a child, I believed that if a man can love a man, he can marry one, too. On that summer night, my mouth tasting a lot like Dove soap, I lay on my bed imagining my wedding to my neighbor and wondering who would wear the dress. I might even have started picking out the Playschool china if our parents had ever let us play together again, which they did not. In that way, I learned two indelible lessons: that there were many kinds of love, and that adults were not crazy about this fact. I was six years old.

Eventually, of course, I did pick out china with a boy, but we live in the world of stubborn grown-ups, not wise children, and the sight of two people in love isn't always received simply or with grace. As my uncles, aunts, cousins, mother, brother, and now Jason and I can attest, sometimes you just have to love first and hope that, eventually, the world sees it for what it is.

5

Flirt, but Don't Touch

OH, TIME. ONE DAY YOU'RE RUSHING TO THE CHURCH IN your wedding clothes, and the next thing you know, you can't even fit into your now-dated duds. The bright-eyed newly-weds you once were have long been replaced by old marrieds who keep to a pleasant, if uneventful, routine. Unquestion-ably, the stability and predictability of home life are comforts worth achieving, yet the resulting domestic bliss can some-times feel like a soporific, lulling lovers to sleep instead of play. Is it any surprise that so many eyes wander in search of excitement and novelty?

There are a number of ways to deal with the fact that the world is full of attractive people and that marriage does not inherently blind you to this knowledge. You can, like Jimmy Carter, admit apologetically that you have "lusted in your heart," making it sound like a shortcoming on your part. You can, alternately, go the seventies-era David Bowie route, and bring home a rock star for your spouse to find naked in your bed. Or you can go to the opposite extreme: follow the advice of many well-intended religious leaders who encourage you to see, hear, and speak no evil, "evil" in this specific case meaning having the hots for people with whom you didn't walk down the aisle.

My grandparents followed the latter course. Or, to be accurate, they didn't speak about something they both could see and hear: my grandfather's flirtatious nature. And their silence came to haunt them.

When I was nine, my grandfather came home from work with an enormous oblong cardboard box. My grandmother did not rush to the door to meet him and, indeed, stood on the other side of what she called "the divider," a sideboard-meets-island that split the kitchen from the dining room. Grampy fumbled to untie the red ribbon on the box she did not reach for and said, "Look, Lula, it's roses." Inside, just as he said, a dozen long-stemmed beauties lay pressed together, waiting for a squeal of delight that never came.

Grampy set the box down on the divider between them, and Grammy, chin jutting forward like the blade of a power tool, said, "You can think again, Mister, if you think I'm touching them things." And with that she disappeared into their room and shut the door. Two very long and very quiet days passed, during which the roses sunk more deeply into their cardboard coffin, before Grampy admitted defeat and removed the offending bouquet from where it had lain untouched.

It was a cousin who clued me in: Grampy had been flirting with the redhead who worked the second checkout line at the A&P market in the next town over. It depends on whom you ask in my family whether he and the shopgirl had actually done anything together. (As a nine-year-old, I did not want to envision my grandfather "doing" anything at all.) Either way, he had been pretending not to find this woman attractive, pretending not to be flirting with her, pretending he didn't notice that his wife, no dummy, had noticed all the pretending. He'd ignored Grammy's growing irritation—which, in a catch-22, he couldn't address without raising the issue of *what* was making her irritated—and she in turn had refused to broach the subject herself. Nobody was talking about what everyone could see. The result was that when things finally did come to a head, it involved angry accusations and recriminations, followed by a box of "I'm sorry" flowers, which proved only that Grampy could badly misjudge Grammy's temperament even after a half century together.

Over the years, I would get conflicting versions of the series of events that led up to the war of the roses. One story, which seemed plausible, was that Grampy had been an outrageous flirt as far back as when he met Grammy while working on her father's farm. Grammy had believed that the combination of their marriage and his conversion to her religion would naturally put a stop to this behavior. It did not, and, in this telling of the story, she would get steamed at the tiniest wink of his eye; his perceived emotional infidelity (not yet accompanied by any physical fall) made her withdraw her affections somewhat. The resulting cooling between them led him to up the ante, crossing new lines in response, which then only wounded her more. The older they got, the more this became a pattern into which they settled, or should I say, hardened.

Would he have cheated on any level if he'd just been free to admit that he was a horny guy? If she had been able to turn his roving eye into a family joke, thereby keeping the subject on the table and not hidden from discussion, might they have turned that into playfulness at home instead of a soap opera at the A&P? I wonder what might have happened if she had found a way to acknowledge his impulses while also setting the limits she could live with: flirt, but don't touch. We'll never know; they were of a generation in which that sort of sexually frank discussion was not encouraged by their families, their faith, or the media. What I do know is that, as a grown-up, the memory of those roses is still a warning: that which you don't speak of will haunt you.

Jason and I have always been very open about the hotties whose paths we cross. We see 'em, speak about 'em, and hear each other's opinion. This has occasionally caught other people off guard. Once on a visit to Grampa Greenwood in Arizona, we went with Jason's relatives to a local family-owned Mexican restaurant just north of the U.S. border. There, Jason and I were both struck by one of the waiters, who was what a friend of mine would call "a snack" (as in, good enough to eat). The hunky son of the owner, The Snack had beautiful eyes, a thick head of dark hair, and a muscular chest poured into a tight T-shirt with the clear intent that no one should miss a detail of his workout. Jason was seated across from me at a long table, and when The Snack came to take our order, I stretched my foot across the distance under the table and kicked Jason, the universal gesture for, "Get a load of *him*!" I needn't have bothered: Jason's eyes were already full of the waiter. To my slight embarrassment, a female relative's eyes were also full—of Jason admiring the waiter.

Over the course of the meal, we both flirted shamelessly with The Snack, who was perfectly receptive in the fashion of anyone who knows he's earning a huge tip from the homos. There was nothing serious going on here; it was just carefree flirtation, with both of us in on the deal. But at one point I saw someone in our party observing us and shaking her head; her husband caught her eye and shrugged as if to say, "I don't get it either." We'd been spotted playing our little game, and, though it was hardly like doing the humpty dance, I did feel a little exposed.

What can I say? We enjoyed what I perceived as a privilege of an all-male marriage: we didn't have to pretend not to get turned on by other people. It would be a generalization to say that in all straight relationships women prefer not to know whom else their boyfriends or husbands check out. And it would be a similarly broad claim to say that all gay couples sit around and chat about who else is on their fantasy playlist. But I have enough female friends to know that many women think of it as borderline freakish how often men think about the bodies moving in space around them. With no one in our relationship to expect that our eyes wouldn't wander, and seeing as both parties had perfectly active male libidos, it would've seemed silly for Jason or me to pretend otherwise. And, besides, with whom else could we talk about the fit of The Snack's one-size-too-small blue jeans? I sure wasn't going to mention it to Grampa Greenwood.

While flirting is fun in itself, *being flirted with* is even better. Yes, Jason and I were both off the proverbial market but it was still flattering to be noticed by the occasional stranger. Actually, it was better to be cruised while married than as a single person, because, for us, it meant there was no follow-through; it was flirting without the nervous interior dialogue about whether this would lead to: a) a great new relationship; b) a nether-regions itch which would require a prescription; or, c) a terri-fying last evening on earth with a madman and his bone-saw.

Any time one of us was cruised without the other present, it became a story to be shared at the dinner table. Once, Jason was driving down the highway when another car began to fol-low him. Jason knew immediately what had attracted the dri-ver's attention: not our car itself, a distinctly unsexy forest green Saturn, but the rainbow sticker on the back bumper. Adorning your car with a symbol universally recognized by gay people can help foster a much-needed sense of pride and community, but it also has the potential drawback of marking you as a target for homophobes who themselves have figured out just what your little sticker represents. As the other car be-gan shadowing Jason, pulling close, then dropping back, he couldn't be sure at first what was going on. Finally the car pulled directly alongside ours, and the driver—a red-headed kid maybe all of twenty—made eye contact with Jason just once, before speeding up and zipping out of sight.

Was the kid a peer or an attacker or just some yahoo into drag racing? Jason didn't give it much more thought, for he was approaching his destination, a crafts store, for what was supposed to a quick trip. But instead of darting in and out, he lingered, caught up in the lure of glitter and felt, until his crafty reverie was interrupted: the young driver—let's call him Red—was standing in the feather boa section, as if waiting for Jason. Much as he liked to flirt, Jason had a brief pang of fear over Red's motives and judiciously moved on to the regis-ters to make the purchases he'd come in for.

But before Jason made it back to the car, Red approached him and stammered nervously, "I saw the . . . um . . . rainbow sticker." There was the briefest of pauses before he blurted out. "Do you have a boyfriend?" My hubby, knowing this was not the time for a discussion of the semantic differences between "boyfriend" and "husband," replied that, yes, he did. Red appeared crestfallen and mumbled, "Oh. I wondered, 'cause you're cute." And with that, the disappointed lad hopped in his car and drove away.

Jason worried a little that he'd been unnecessarily abrupt. For all he knew, it might have taken great courage for Red to speak to him—after all, it required both a round of highway tag and ten minutes lurking in the feather boa aisle to work up his nerve to speak. But there was nothing else appropriate for Jason to do except go on his way and then drive home as fast as he could to tell me that he'd been hit on by a younger man. This tale was proof that, despite the march of time, he still had it. And isn't that what we all want?

I was cruised less often than Jason because I represent— and let me say this in a way that is neither too self-deprecating nor likely to invoke the wrath of Fat Rights advocates—a somewhat more specialized taste. Your average gay man is just like your average straight man in one regard: he does not think flab is sexy. Sure, there are men of all stripes who like an ample figure, but it's not any more the norm in gay culture than in American culture at large. And I learned early on that my shape, more Santa than surfer dude, was not a hot commodity. Even Jason had to get used to my body when we began dating, and he at least had the benefit of attaching my personality to the package. But sometimes, to my eternal surprise and great delight, someone who didn't have that advantage still made sure to let me know that I was—ho ho ho—just what he liked.

At the end of one semester, I was sitting in a coffee shop holding student conferences when a butch military guy approached me. I had seen him there before, part of the crowd of regulars, but because he was older than my students, I didn't know whether he was a student or a faculty member. I thought of him as GI Joe, for obvious reasons. On that day, GI Joe came to my table and asked if he was right in guessing that I was a writing professor. He told me he'd been impressed over the previous weeks with how I seemed to know all my students as individuals. Without waiting for an invitation to sit, he turned a chair around and straddled it, then told me about himself. He had been in the military for years, was on leave while the government paid for a college degree, and was looking forward to his return to active duty. I was about to ask what he was studying when he lowered his voice and got to the point. "I wish I was a student of yours," he said hoarsely. I dumbly asked why and he leaned in to answer, "'Cause then *I'd* have your attention."

Whoo baby. I'm assuming GI Joe had to embrace "Don't ask, don't tell" and keep this exchange to himself. But I was under no such obligation, and you can bet I was eager to brag about our interaction. I was especially gloaty because I knew that Jason would be jealous that a big meaty army stud had tried to hook me with a husky come-on—it was like the start of a porn flick but without the cheesy synthesizer music.

Being able to talk about such moments helped take the edge off of them. By *edge* I mean that crackle of sexual energy that arises from the unknown—something hard to maintain when you actually live with another person. It's not exactly a secret that it's difficult to keep things fresh physically with someone you've been intimate with for years. This difficulty results from a confluence of factors, like having long ago memorized your husband's default positions, but also now associating him with decidedly unhot things like leaving his underwear on the hall floor until you pick it up. You can still be having sex with your partner and enjoying it, but it's tough to replicate that initial sensation of second-to-second discovery possible with a new partner. That's what keeps flirting so electric: the memory of a time when a lover's body was an undiscovered country.

To pretend that only home is where the hard-on is, then, seems like a way to set yourself up for needless frustration and a useless loop of denial. Being able, instead, to admit you are turned on by others without actually acting on it strikes me as a key to making a relationship last. For if you never talk to the person you married about this one area of your feelings, or if your spouse is truly horrified that you even *have* such feelings, the whole subject is going to go underground— and that's a dangerous place for it to be. People who can't even get *verbal* release may well seek other ways to let it all out.

Some would say that the answer is to have open relationships. There has always been a strong contingent in the gay community that promotes mutually agreed-upon adultery as a sex-positive way of keeping things fresh while promoting true intimacy; this camp sees monogamy as dated and unnatural, both a tool of oppression and a recipe for disaster. And it's not just sodomites waving this banner, thank you. The "free love" pendulum swings, so to speak, through the straight world with regularity, from the key-party seventies to the turn of the millennium, where "negotiated non-monogamy" has become a hot subject for the Craig's List set. This approach, mind you, blows Jason's and my swapping of flirty stories out of the water: it's quite a leap from being open about your feelings to openly feeling others up.

One of the first gay couples I knew had a committed open relationship. They were both professionals, then working in separate cities, so this arrangement had a certain logic. Sleeping with the occasional cutie didn't involve messy elements like sneaking around or making up stories about why the UPS guy had no pants on. I found it a little unsettling, I admit, mostly because I wasn't sure I would like such an arrangement for myself. But, like most of my reactions, that was about me; as for them, they'd made their plan work for years and seemed perfectly content.

That is, until they weren't. When they actually lived in the same city, there was more tension. This was perhaps unavoidable. Your partner's presence in another bed is more potent when you are expecting him home in yours. Plus, the closer in proximity you are to the evidence of your partner's affairs, the more concrete the matter becomes. It's suddenly much easier to lie awake pondering just what diseases you are now one degree removed from—for, no matter how much you trust your partner, how do you trust the other party, someone you don't even know? I imagine the questions piling up: how many nights out constitute more than just a fling? And despite a couple's stated contract to keep affairs on the purely physical level, is there really any way to guarantee the absence of emotion, the fuel that powers the human machine?

Flirt as we might like, Jason and I never even tried to pull off the whole open relationship thing. I'm a hopeless mushball: I equate sex with love (so retro, I know, but there it is), and if

I had an affair, I would too easily invest my new relationship with emotional meaning completely disproportionate to the actual situation. Jason knows this about me, and, as much as he'd be excited at the prospect of himself getting to have an affair just to balance out mine, it would make him insanely jealous to think my heart was leaping for someone else.

So we always limited our adventures to the ocular variety. Ninety-nine percent of the time, this was effortless and amusing; but on rare occasions, our openness required a little more fancy footwork. Once, Jason met a guy at work who was startlingly like him: a gay baker-schoolteacher who was into cycling, a new passion of Jason's. When I met Cycle Boy myself, I agreed with Jason that the guy was not only handsome but a great catch all-around: smart, funny, and financially secure. I even joked that I could see how Cycle Boy would make an ideal romantic replacement for me should my worst phobia— being crushed by a falling crane—ever come true.

When Jason and Cycle Boy started hanging out more, I did have little pangs, but only little ones, until Jason raised the idea of their taking a week-long bicycle trip together through Vermont. As I don't bike, I wouldn't be going along, and so my heretofore latent jealousy kicked in, aided by my writer's imagination. I had visions of them pulling off the road by some goat farm, only to discover an inviting pond to cool down in, which would naturally require them to slowly strip out of their bike gear, unveiling ride-pumped, glistening limbs which would soon intertwine in a blaze of man passion that would melt the chèvre for miles around.

That was a wild scenario, to be sure, but I did know my husband, and I could tell he was attracted to Cycle Boy. If I'd followed Grammy's model, I wouldn't have said anything at all, letting my worries fester until something happened. But I had learned the lesson of those roses, and so I took a deep breath one night as we cooked dinner and said, "You have a crush on this guy, huh?" Jason grinned, a little sheepish, and said he did. The door to this topic was now open, and so we kept walking through it. I told him my visions of his roadside idylls and he told me he'd had a few visions himself—which he also said he would never act on. This led the discussion beyond him and Cycle Boy. For the first time in our marriage, we really talked about whether or not we would ever cheat on each other.

We acknowledged that sometimes we each fantasized about outside trysts. And we discussed that while we knew, at least theoretically, that open relationships worked for some, we had to accept who *we* were: one easily attached and the other easily made jealous—the worst possible combination for partner-swapping. We agreed that we would continue to remain faithful. But, along the way, we would still compare notes on the men who made us stand at attention.

The agreement we made in that kitchen, which time would eventually test, was never about right or wrong. It was only about the people involved and what would work best for our marriage. For all the stimulation provided by snacky waiters, army studs, and cycling buddies, what really mattered was making sure we took care of our union in a way that meant that there would always be someone waiting at home to tell our stories to.

6

Miffing

You hear a lot of truisms about relationships as you grow up: "Love means never having to say you're sorry." "Never go to bed angry." "Someone has to compromise." Everyone knows the first one is bullshit from a drippy seventies movie, but the other two have some real traction in the world of marital advice. That Jason and I were good at both of the latter principles is less a credit to the brilliance of our relationship than to the thoroughness with which such advice is marketed to poor, foolish souls embarking on the journey of marriage. In fact, we were observing one dictum too many for our relationship to be anywhere near as healthy as we thought.

As we approached our "wood anniversary"—that's five years, as anyone in Grammy's generation knew—one of the things I was most proud of was how harmonious our relationship was. Because no one ever saw us fight, or even engage in the petty emotional sabotage some couples like to display in public settings, more than once friends asked if we ever fought and, if so, how we handled it. I would always shrug and say, "We don't fight; we miff." I said this as innocently as I could, pretending that I didn't know that this made us sound so delightfully above the fray.

Not everyone uses "miff" as a verb in quite this way. You might say that you *get* miffed or that your actions end up miffing someone else. But Jason and I *miff*, a dual-action verb in which we simultaneously piss each other off. It works like this: he'll say, "Why the hell can't you ever shut a drawer that you've opened?" and I'll say, "I'll answer that question when you remember to put a dirty glass in the sink for once in your life." This is followed by mutual eye-rolling, perhaps a groan of some kind, and that's that. There you have a taste of every Valdes Greenwood fight for years: short, stupid, and easily forgotten.

If our miffs were going to happen somewhere, it was most likely to be in the kitchen, and often the subject was utensils. Before my husband, I'd had no idea that abiding moral outrage can be stirred up, if you will, by one's choice of spoon. I am, by the standards of many unions, a decent cook, but I am neither as skilled nor as intuitive in the kitchen as Jason. Unfortunately, I rarely read a recipe all the way through before I begin cooking, which means I often discover too late that there is some tricky element or difficult technique that I am entirely unprepared for. Jason would think of this a test of his skill; I react like a man exposed to bird flu—recoil, panic, scramble for solution, and worry about the outcome.

That's how I felt when I was making an almond glaze for a tart one night and came upon the warning that if it ever came to a boil, even for a few seconds, the liquid would settle into an "undesirable corn-flake–like consistency," which would "mar the attractiveness of the final product." Ack! After the initial wave of panic subsided, I determined that there was no way I was going to mar this baby. I turned the flame low enough to yield the merest simmer, and, for good measure, was going to gently stir the mixture to further keep the boiling at bay.

Poised to stir, I was stopped by Jason's voice, which contained a note of horror. "You're not really using that spoon, are you?" This was a rhetorical question: the spoon, long and metal, was halfway to the pot when he stopped me; clearly, yes, I had planned to use this spoon and, clearly, he was aghast that I would do such a thing. He would never use a metal spoon in a situation that so obviously called for a wooden one. But he couldn't just say so, or perhaps gently offer me a better utensil with a helpful explanation; he needed to play out the minidrama of his dismay while my almond glaze bubbled toward cornflakedom.

My response, inevitably blending sarcasm and self-righteousness, was to point out how lucky he was that I was willing to make a tart that came with a warning and, moreover, that if he wasn't happy with the result, he could always *not* eat it. Sensing danger if he continued, Jason merely rolled his eyes, tossed me a farewell "whatever," and vacated the kitchen while the first cornflakes appeared in my glaze.

These food fights were most likely to occur before friends came over for dinner, as happened every weekend. Jason and I have never focused much on material goods, preferring instead to emphasize life experiences, and that most often meant cooking for people we loved. If Rumpelstiltskin could spin gold from straw, we could make ours from short ribs and coconut cake. Entertaining was our currency, and, if you know that old saw about how couples fight most about money, it's no wonder every dinner party caused us to miff like mad.

Each second closer to the guests' arrival would ratchet things up. Jason might hog the good cutting board, or I might decide to arrange flowers in the sink just as he needed to drain the pasta. Such moments occasioned little conversation; it's surprising how few syllables are required to let your spouse know he's miffing you off. For a while, we tried allowing only one person in the kitchen at a time, but we always were planning too big a meal for such a strategy to be practical. So it was miff, chop, miff, stir, miff. Fortunately, this predinner theater had no audience. Our guests never saw the show. For at the sound of the doorbell, Jason and I would become the home team again, eager to welcome visitors who would only see the smiles of the ever-serene couple they had come to expect.

Because this was the low-level argument we most typically had, it was fairly easy to keep up with the second truism: never go to bed angry. Most of the time, if something was bugging us, we just hashed it out at the dinner table. We're one of those couples who sit down to dinner together every night to share amusing tales of the day (on good days) and our grievances (on bad days). With bedtime yet hours away, this gives us plenty of time to clear the air and even come back for round two of a heated discussion long before settling in for the night.

In five years, I had only broken the never-sleep-angry rule once. The night in question was supposed to have been a good one. As an early-career playwright, I'd been excited to have a staged reading coming up at the Boston Center for the Arts. But ten days before, I'd realized that an entire act of my play stunk. I mean, hold your nose and say *"pew."* Panicked, I wrote eighteen hours a day for two days straight to yield thirty new pages of text. Every day, I ran into the theater with page substitutions, until the cast complained of carpal tunnel syndrome from endlessly highlighting text. Then, when one actor quit after the fourth read-through, his role was recast overnight with only two rehearsals left. By opening night of a three-night run, I was nervous, sure that I was about to reveal myself to the world as a hack.

Every field has its protocols and traditions, and in the theater world, if you love someone you show up with flowers on opening night. In our years together, I had added another element to this ritual: I expected Jason not only to bring flowers, but to be there in plenty of time to calm down his nervous husband. On that night, I paced around the theater lobby feeling sick to my stomach and trying to make positive-sounding small talk with audience members, but Jason was nowhere in sight. The theater flashed the lobby lights, and still no Jason. My first instinct, learned from my grandmother's habit of living life as a perpetual widow's walk, was to imagine him dead or wounded somewhere. But when he rushed in as the lights were blinked for the final time, my concern for his well-being was replaced with that kind of relieved annoyance that comes from waiting for someone who has now proven that he has no mortally convincing excuse for his tardiness. It didn't help that he wasn't trailing blossoms in his wake—he had come empty-handed.

All that aside, the reading went very well. The actors were totally on and the audience vocal in its appreciation. Later, at home, I crawled into bed a relieved and happy man and would have fallen asleep in this condition, except that Jason asked if he could give me his opinion of the new material in the script.

It was 1:30 a.m., so perhaps I just wasn't thinking, but I said yes. Jason may not be a writer but he is a tough audience: he has an astute critical eye, with which he had spotted—and was now pointing out to the playwright in bed with him—a huge organic flaw in the revision. I'd even briefly considered the existence of the problem he described, but had made peace with it due to the shortness of time. But now, when I should've been basking in the glow of a successful evening, The Flaw had been invoked aloud.

With The Flaw lying between Jason and me like the Great Wall, I passed the night awake, silently compiling a litany of his errors: showing up late, which I saw as being unsupportive; coming empty-handed, which seemed cold; and then blithely announcing, at bedtime no less, that my script had a huge problem visible even to someone without theater training. I fumed without letting him know that I was. I let him go to sleep thinking I had been perfectly mature about his feedback, when in fact I was calling him all sorts of terrible names in my head. All that sleepless night, my anger loomed over me.

In the morning, I was surly. Let something fester, even overnight, and it's like letting bread rise: the same amount of material can double in size. Forget miffing, I was spoiling for a fight. I made no pleasantries, avoided eye contact, and I didn't join in when Jason sang out a showtune line about bagels. (Note: a gay man weaned on Sondheim, he can dredge up a showtune line about just about anything, and, if one doesn't exist, he'll make one up, complete with rhymes.) When he finally asked if I was mad, while unwisely patting me like a pet, I let him have it, ticking off my complaints. He tried to hug the irritation out of me, but—and this is the problem with any gripe unvented overnight—I was unable to relinquish a grudge nurtured so carefully over long dark hours.

That night, I went alone to the theater, sat through a second performance, and emerged unscathed: The Flaw did not end the world and the audience was again enthusiastic. When I tip-toed into our apartment afterwards, quietly creeping past the bedroom, where Jason was sleeping, and into the kitchen, there on the table was the biggest bouquet of flowers I'd ever received, with a note: *"Late for the play, late with the flowers, early with the criticism. Sorry."*

I have often recounted that story, a sweet tale which proves the truth of the bedtime maxim, as well as the lie of never having to say you're sorry. But neither of those old saws involved the more complicated terrain of the third truism that I had grown up believing, the one about compromise. That's where the "we-only-miff" couple got stuck.

Ideally, of course, compromise—a key to all negotiations, business or personal—would come from both sides equally. But I had often heard that in most relationships one person is the real peacekeeper who knows when to compromise for the sake of harmony. In our relationship, I was clearly this party, and while I didn't always love being the one to ameliorate things, I did kind of enjoy thinking of myself as a sort of emotional UN secretary-general. I never thought to examine whether it really counts as compromise when it's always the same person giving in. And Jason figured if I was happy with this arrangement, he was in no hurry to question it.

The single biggest reason we only "miffed" and seldom seriously argued was that I took my peacekeeper role to heart far too often. Jason and I didn't see eye-to-eye on many things, but when push came to shove, I always asked myself what was worth getting heated over and what could be lived without. Our relationship provided me so many things, certainly I could give up this or that to keep the peace.

Here's a prime example: I love movies and Jason doesn't. Unfettered, I would see a movie or two every single week of the year in the theater. Jason couldn't see the appeal of this obsession of mine, because he didn't share it. This should have been a matter of simple difference, but it irked him that I didn't respond to his disapproval with some new restraint. First, he approached it as a money issue: could I really afford seeing so many movies? But it was his next tack that won me over: he made my movie-going about our relationship. How, he asked, could I just run off to whatever film caught my fancy without any regard for whether he wanted to see it with me? He'd never get to films alone; with his job, he couldn't go to matinees and was too tired to go out afterward. He reserved weekend days for cycling, which left only weekend evenings—when we weren't entertaining—as our likely movie-going option. So why couldn't I just wait till then? Didn't I *want* to spend to time with him?

Emotions are my Achilles heel, and no one wants to be a selfish bastard, right? So I suggested what I called a compromise: I would list the films that opened each week and he'd say which two or three films he wanted me to wait to see, both of us knowing it would be an effort to convince him to go to even one in the coming week. As the next week's films opened, the list of wait-for-me movies would grow, and eventually, in my effort to keep the peace, I missed many films I'd waited months to see while Jason forgot all about them.

I failed to recognize that this was not actually compromise, but capitulation. What he valued set the pace and, on the pretense that a matter like movie-going was of little consequence, I gave in. What I called meeting him halfway was actually me finding a way to feel okay about doing what he wished.

From that victory forward, the same technique could be applied broadly. Even our bedtime routine bore out this pattern: he wanted to read in bed, and not on the couch, while I was trying to sleep. I claimed this was insensitive because he knew that I was a light sleeper; he argued that if he gave in, wouldn't that reflect my insensitivity to his need to wind down? You can guess who won; in this case, I didn't even fake a compromise—I literally rolled over.

With the remove of time, I can see that we simply didn't know how to fight. We valued the same thing at bottom—harmony in our relationship—but didn't know how to make that possible if we didn't always want the same things along the way. It's certainly not as if either of us had great models of conflict resolution to look to. Both sets of our parents divorced, which didn't offer much useful instruction for relationship maintenance. And neither of our families was especially vocal: Grammy framed every complaint through sighs and a Bible verse; my mother never raised her voice at all. Jason's dad just goes quiet for lengthy periods of time and his mom's side of the family is soft-spoken by nature.

I'm not saying it's a good thing to come from a family that shouts and hollers, or to be like those people who let it all fly and then apologize afterwards. There are distinct soul-preserving attributes to not calling each other an asshole every time the word pops to mind (which is a lot in five years). But we just didn't know how to both hold our ground and then deal directly with the conflicts that would naturally arise because of it. And so we did what seemed the best possible thing: we masked our tensions with alleged compromises, and patted ourselves on the back for our maturity.

Nobody's perfect, especially a young couple finding their way. Our early years of genial agreement may have given us depth to stand up to the tests ahead. Or perhaps they were setting us up for the fall to come. At the time, I only knew that when I crawled into bed at night, I was convinced that I wasn't really angry, just a little miffed that the damn light was still on.

Crossing the Threshold

7

The Missing DINK

CLEVER READERS MAY WELL BE ASKING THEMSELVES A FAIR question: where's the baby? Remember the old line about a Chekov play: if a gun shows up in the first act, you can be sure it's going to go off eventually. One could logically expect that a baby discussed so prominently on our second date might well show up at this point, five years into our marriage. So why no baby? Well, let's just say life is not as precise as a Chekov play.

When Jason and I had moved in together in 1994, we had made three folders that corresponded with our future plans: wedding, house-buying, and adoption, in that order. Soon after we created these folders, we pulled off a lovely wedding, an accomplishment which made us fairly confident that the other elements would follow in timely fashion. But the truth is that we'd only spent $3,000 on the whole wedding and $2,000 of that was paid for by Jason's father and stepmother. There is a big difference between our having scrounged up the remaining thousand bucks for our wedding and actually being able to buy a house on our own—which we were determined to do before we talked seriously about children.

How could we have expected that after five years of hard work since our wedding, we would essentially be right where we started? It was 2000 and I was back teaching part time at Emerson, Jason was still working with preschoolers, and we were still renting the apartment we'd moved into a few months after getting married. Granted, Jason's pay rose with inflation each year, but the rent had also gone up over time; meanwhile, the college was still paying me in magic beans, with which I had to buy costly health insurance for myself. It's not as if Jason and I were slackers; we were both working diligently and excelling in our classrooms, but we still didn't seem to be advancing noticeably upward financially.

Part of the problem was that we chose to live in the Boston area, justly notorious for its cost of housing. We lived in an allegedly two-bedroom apartment which, at $900 in the year 2000, was considered a steal; though the average cost of a similar apartment that year was $600 in Boise, and $750 in Vegas, the average Boston two-bed was over a thousand bucks, with many nonluxury units hitting $1,100–$1,200. Meanwhile, unlike in other parts of the country where a two-bedroom apartment comes with two actual bedrooms—and maybe even two baths—in Boston a "two-bed" typically meant one bedroom and a dining room which, if we replaced table and chairs with a mattress and nightstand, could pretend to be a second bedroom; as for second baths, well, that sort of thing was for rich folk in swank seaport lofts downtown. Our "two-bed" was simply four rooms which we were allowed to configure at will—hell, if we didn't want a living room either, it was a three-bed.

This stunning value came with terrific period detail: the ancient floorboards beneath our kitchen sink were rotting from a leaky pipe that the landlord had fixed with tape and a towel. The bathroom ceiling was badly water-stained from where a stream had actually broken through before the landlord had solved the problem. The combination of deeply scarred wood flooring and the stained off-yellow walls only added to the impression that we were living inside the face of an elderly diner waitress who smoked too much. To be honest, we passed the place off as having a kind of bohemian splendor, and friends thought we had a good deal going. But the true caliber of the place for which we were paying $11,000 a year can best be summed up by this: its windows were so old, so rotted and perfunctory, that we had to shrink-wrap them to get through the winter.

For people who do not live in cold climates where the housing stock is old, that sentence may have no meaning at all. But in New England, the bone-cracking cold of winter and the abusive seasons in general take quite a toll on traditional wooden window frames and sills. In too many homes, the windows barely hang onto the walls, seemingly too lazy to actually fall out on the ground, but also too exhausted to preclude winds from sweeping inside the house. New homeowners in these parts often replace the windows immediately as both a quality of life issue and an investment for resale; many landlords, however, shrug off the whole window issue, figuring there will never be as many crappy apartments as people desperate to get them. Renters, then, at the bottom of the food chain, have three basic options: wearing layers (think fleece over hoodie over henley); going to the store to buy plastic window wrap; or hypothermia, which at the very least puts an end to renting.

Each year that we lived in that apartment, Jason and I took advantage of both nonlethal options: bundling up at home and also making an annual pilgrimage to Ace Hardware to buy plastic sheeting. There were a surprising number of brands to choose from: some came with special tape to affix to the window frame, and some, designed for fools, allegedly just clung to the glass. If we'd wanted, we could have even gone the heavy duty DYI route, buying bolts of plastic sheeting to staple-gun into place. One especially imaginative element of the brand we used was that once the plastic was affixed, the instructions commanded us to blow dry it, so that it could more firmly seal and protect our apartment from upcoming blizzards. In most places, two gay guys with hair dryers would indicate a salon, not the onset of winter, but late autumn always found us wielding handheld blowers like power tools inside our apartment.

Don't get the wrong idea, though. I've done poor—think charity clothing and powdered milk—and this was not it. As far as I was concerned, if we could afford Boston rent prices with enough money left over to wrap our place like a Christo installation, we were middle class. Jason was doubtful about this claim and much less comfortable than I was with our perpetual rentalhood. Every year as we waited to see whether our rent would rise or not, he complained, "Renting is like flushing money down the drain. All that money gone and nothing to show." At the same time, he wasn't about to become a banker, nor did he have any plans for making us millionaires. All he could do was look for ways to cut corners and try to get ahead somehow—which also meant convincing me that "better than poverty" was not an especially lofty aspiration.

The shrink-wrapping was supposed to help. Except that after the first winter it was clear to me that the plastic wrap, which took forever to get mounted, wasn't very effective at combating the dogged winds. Drafts didn't creep into the rooms so much as stride in boldly, and the house constantly felt cold as a result. My idea of a fix was to blast the heat; I was willing to do the window sheeting so that we weren't overtly heating the outdoors, but that seemed conservative enough to me. If I was going to live in a plastic bubble, I figured I could at least be warm while doing so. In contrast, Jason saw this as a matter of fiscal responsibility: if the plastic wasn't going to keep the furnace from kicking in too often, then we'd just have to put the thermostat on a timer. This way, although the apartment still looked mummified, heating it wasn't going to bankrupt us.

In this manner, we simply kept to the roles we had assumed since the beginning of our marriage: Jason, the Jack Sprat of spending, and I, the wife. Jason is no miser, just very cautious; he doesn't like to spend money that he could use later when he really needs something. Compromising my Sprat analogy, though, is the fact that when the moment finally comes that Jason is ready for a purchase, he's burdened with champagne taste, leading him to spend enough to eclipse the savings from his past frugality. My taste is less rarefied than his; I have a chip in my brain that acts like a homing device for sales. Ordinarily, this would help us get ahead, except that I routinely render my discounts nil by buying three "bargains" at once.

Over the years, then, a pattern emerged. If I knew we needed something for the home, I'd start off looking for the best deal, while he'd be looking for the finest product. When Jason began teaching himself the fine art of pastry-making several years after we married, I knew he wanted a serious standing mixer. I found a hardware-store brand on sale, a vast improvement over the hand mixer we were using, but he sniffed, "I'd rather wait for a KitchenAid." Then, when our very eighties food processor died, he couldn't just replace it with any old thing: he wanted a Cuisinart. In both cases, he couldn't bring himself to part with enough cash to buy the item he wanted; people who didn't own a house couldn't justify such purchases, he argued. But he continued to want them and, in the kitchen equivalent of making up for my impoverished childhood by blasting the heat, I eventually bought him both. It wasn't quite instant gratification, but gratifying nonetheless: the boy who grew up on welfare cheese felt like a good provider; the guy who valued quality and frugality received the former while not technically sacrificing the latter himself.

I say technically because, while I was the one making the purchases, the checks were written from the only bank account I had: the one we shared. From soon after we married, we had pooled both our incomes into one joint checking account. Many other couples wisely keep their finances entirely separate as a way of preserving individual responsibility and avoiding the pitfalls that can arise from two very different people envisioning how best to use the same money. But we were young and idealistic, so joint checking seemed very much in the spirit of for-richer-for-poorer.

Despite our different tacks toward spending, we never got too heated in our talks about money because we never thought of ourselves as actually having any. Theoretically, as DINKs—

a "double income no kid" couple—we should have been rolling in all the dough we were saving by not having to buy formula and diapers. And we kept reading right-wing propaganda that said we gays had enormous amounts of disposable income. But, like many of our Boston peers without MBAs, we always seemed to have just enough to afford living where we did, with a little left over from time to time. If we already weren't getting ahead, why risk upsetting the delicate balance of our checkbook by trying to buy a house? The whole notion of home buying seemed so extravagant, so beyond our means, that it became easier to spend for the moment, not the future. When we earned a little extra or got a little bit ahead, we did what the young and unthinking do: we spent it.

If Jason was going to make some enormous purchase (enormous meaning it involved a whopping four figures), it would be an item like his bicycle, which cost nearly twice as much as our monthly rent. My biggest expense was a trip to Alaska one summer to attend a theatre festival where one of my plays would be performed. True to form, while Jason was likely to spend money on an item from which he would get many years' use, I chose an event that lasted only a week. Still, I told myself it would advance my playwriting career, which might earn us money in the future. Granted, the idea of spending hard-earned money to earn future drama royalties is like watering your garden with champagne to raise ragweed, but I was desperate for any chance to promote my work.

The conference was in Valdez, Alaska, and playwrights would have to fly themselves there, pay for a week's housing and a week's food, and even pay full price for the conference. For me, the cost of the festival quickly rose to $2,000. No one but the writers was paying that much to attend: everyone else involved got either free food, free housing, free or discounted admission, or all of the above. But I was determined to go and make the most of what was billed as a development opportunity. Unfortunately, it was clear almost from the moment I arrived that this "investment" in my career was really just going to be a money drain. The unrehearsed cast performed before an audience of about twenty people in the middle of an afternoon, and the expected "development" turned out to be three panelists fielding a few questions before moving on to the next show.

I am not one to easily admit that I have been a rube. I can fess up if I've done something wrong or hurt someone's feelings, yet I hate to acknowledge looking foolish. But there I was, a guy who spent his winters living inside what appeared to be a snow globe, and I had spent several months' rent on a naked waste of time.

I called Jason on the far side of the continent each day, sharing my disillusionment, until one night, after I'd detected a distinct coolness in his voice, it hit me: here I was, two thousand bucks down to begin with, and I was racking up the toll calls like they were nothing.

On the three-flight, fifteen-hour trip home, I promised myself I would be a better steward of my—no, *our*—finances. We could do better at saving our savings. I told myself it was time to stop acting like the poor kid I once was, spending whatever cash I got because I was sure it would go away. Maybe I even meant it.

By the time I got back to Boston, my mind was a murky fog. Landing on terra firma only meant I had to begin the next trek, taking a shuttle bus and three subway trains to get to our apartment. I was jet-lagged, bleary-eyed, and limply dragging my luggage up the sidewalk when I saw our landlord, master of tape-and-towel, on the steps of the house.

He "hated to do it," he said before I could even process that he was talking to me, but he had to raise the rent, for only the second time in five years. But this time, instead of going up in a gentle increment, it was going up $200 at once. I found myself swaying unsteadily, half from jet lag and half from shock. Our crappy $11,000 apartment was about to become a crappy $13,000 apartment. The landlord seemed concerned at my condition and tried to speak gently. We had a month to decide whether we still wanted the place and, if we did not, our lease was up two months later. As he drove away in his Jaguar, I stood there on the porch, for a moment unable to compose myself enough to unlock our front door.

When I finally got inside, the apartment was empty and dark. I sank down onto the couch, fully intending to sit there in the gloom until Jason arrived. When my eyes adjusted to the semidark, they settled on the windows, where a sticky ribbon of plastic we'd somehow failed to remove in the spring dangled from the corner of one pane. Harmless little irritant, it had remained there for months and neither of us had ever noticed or cared enough to do anything about it; on that day, it goaded me.

When Jason got home and heard the news, he blanched, swore, and then dropped onto the couch next to me. But we didn't have a fight, and we didn't even miff, because on this we were agreed: we had to put up or shut up. Instead of complaining about shrink wrap, we had to finally take responsibility for our living conditions. We had no idea how we'd do it, much less in three months, but it was finally time to break out folder number two: home buying.

8

Bath, Bed, and Beyond

Is it just me, or is buying a house so stressful and conflict-inducing that once you and your sweetie have actually found a place you can stand to live in, you have no interest in sharing it with each other? It's a singular irony of the process that it makes you dream of separate vacations instead of living together. (Though, after the down payment, vacations are out of the question, as are new clothes or anything Venti at Starbucks.)

Granted, it's not as if we had much choice. Fortunately, our landlord, a nice man despite his disinterest in home maintenance, allowed us an extra two months, which gave us five months to find a place, get a bid accepted, and arrange for a closing date that would have us moved on time to avoid an extra month's rent. This is not the shortest housing search ever, but it did feel a bit crazed, considering we had not yet gotten any prequalifying done, nor did we have the down payment in hand. Newbies that we were, we didn't know how much a down payment would be.

Our first experience with the humanoid life form known as a "mortgage broker" helped us accomplish all three things. We were soon preapproved for so much money, that—had we taken it—we would've become the poster children for foreclosure. Feeling all savvy, we politely declined to borrow beyond our means and settled on a loan amount capped at $150,000. Lyra, as I'll call our broker for reasons implicit, outfoxed our conservative strategy by telling us that, as first-time buyers, we could purchase with only 5 percent down—though she neglected to mention that this would result in private mortgage insurance, increasing the monthly cost of the mortgage we were trying to keep small. Blissfully unaware of that detail, we now knew what our down payment would be: $7,500. Add the $1,200 Lyra said we'd need for closing costs and, just to be safe, we figured we'd need a total of $10,000 to snag a new home. We started looking before we had mapped out where the ten grand would come from.

The first day we visited listed properties in our price range, we trooped into basements and attics, peering at saggy ceilings and trying to block out the smell of cat piss. It soon became clear that sticking to a housing budget of $150,000 in our housing market was like saying you'll only buy diamonds you can pay for in spare change. House by house, we had trouble finding even cubic zirconia on our budget. Short of leaving Metro Boston, we simply weren't going to get much for our money.

That posed a problem. I'm a pedestrian, as in, a nondriver, and not just when I'm on foot. I never got a license, have only had a few driving lessons ever, and have long nursed a surety that I would be a danger to society if I were ever to drive. That means I need to live somewhere on public transportation lines, which means not straying too far from the city. Of course, if you live very close to a subway stop, the price of your housing is markedly higher than it would be further from a train. My primary restriction came with its own conundrum: how do we buy an on-transportation house with an off-transportation budget?

And I wasn't done yet. I had one other request: I needed to have a coffee shop close enough to walk to. I know that hardly sounds like a deal breaker. Would it really kill me to be latte-free if it got us a house? But the fact of the matter is that I am a writer and we writers have superstitions: once you learn how/when/where you write best, you honor that. If you don't, some musey superpower grants you a decade of writer's block. I'm really only half joking about that. I knew that I wrote better in public and, well, coffee shops were where I wrote best of all.

For years, first drafts of every play, feature article, or column I wrote had been generated at Diesel Café in Davis Square. There, baby dykes and gay boys served up coffee, college students played pool, and we writer types hunched over our laptops, both soaking in the scene and completely ignoring it all. I loved Diesel like it was a second home: I would sink happily into my spot on laptop row (inside left wall, just beyond the counter), letting the hubbub wash over me like white noise, as I wrote for hours. Some people go to the sea for inspiration, or to remote cabins; well, chatter was my ocean, and a red Pleather booth my retreat. In contrast, if I sat at home to write, I might wander around picking up the clutter trail, or answer the phone, or watch *The Rosie O'Donnell Show*: too many options.

So there were my demands: near a train and a coffee shop. Surely doable, right? As for Jason, he had fantasies of a condo—and by the end of the first day, we knew it would be a condo—with a fireplace, or a kitchen with lots of cupboards. He hoped for yard access and parking, and he wouldn't have been averse to either a Colonial or a big, open modern loft. But truth be told, he mainly wanted to buy. Period. The whole giving-up-our-lease thing was freaking him out, invoking as it did the undercurrent of imagined homelessness, the deeply unsettling prospect of losing one place before finding the next.

The result on our dispositions was very *Freaky Friday*: we swapped our financial personalities. Jason would see a place, perhaps nearly recoil from it, and then still wonder if it was a fixer-upper we could afford. He could veer dangerously close to becoming a Realtor's dream, able to argue that a butcher block would make a fabulous dining room table and the utensil drawer would be a *lovely* bassinette. Against his typically frugal nature, he could spin himself into a complete buy-now-or-beg-later panic.

Meanwhile, I suddenly had no urge to spend. After I obsessively researched and compared all listed condos within miles, making sure we got in five or six appointments in a day, I would absolutely refuse to commit to any of the properties. I'm such a welfare baby that the asking prices, even in our range, simply paralyzed me. As a result, he could see a condo and think "How much should we bid?" while I'd be thinking "How soon can I nap?"

Sometimes, we were in perfect agreement. Like when we entered the Very Dark Condo, in which the low ceilings and small rooms were not enough—all the floors had forest green carpeting, which matched the triple layers of heavy drapes. All of that could have been dealt with, were it not for the way a filling station backed into the yard, or the general moistness in the air and walls and floors. I don't remember who first invoked the term "mold," but I get queasy just thinking of the whole untended terrariumness of it all. We passed.

Then there was the four-hundred-plus-square-foot cottage that turned out to be literally in the backyard of another house; it offered a sum total of three rooms (two not tall enough for Jason to stand comfortably upright in) and, in a depressing coincidence, was also decked out in forest green, though accented with many dozens of sunflowers. It was like an overgrown dollhouse for a doll with terrible taste. After we drove away with no intention of ever returning, the Realtor actually called to berate us for not bidding on the place. This served only to convince us that many Realtors, like mortgage brokers, are not so much human beings as humanoids. (Will either of those sale-driven species ever embrace humanity all the way? Perhaps it's best if they do not, for their requisite souls would hurt so very much upon the kind of self-examination that the rest of us are given to.)

Meanwhile, as week after week of dispiriting excursions passed, we were cobbling together money. I managed to add a summer class to my teaching schedule and accepted every freelance article assignment that came my way; Jason took on private speech therapy clients. And, to keep Alaska from being a complete drain, I applied for and received a travel grant that retroactively covered part of my expenses for that trip, which already seemed a distant memory. Before we knew it, we were halfway to a down payment. The only problem was finding something to apply that money toward.

As our nerves grew more frayed, I began to accept that I would have to give up at least one of my conditions. It seemed that I was not to have any chance of living near a subway; I might be able to live on a commuter rail line, likely limiting my travel to the hourly schedule, or perhaps on a bus line, which I was averse to because I could picture snowy day after snowy day, with me standing on a curb and cursing my fate as I waited for the bus to lumber into view. Either prospect made me nervous, for I didn't like the idea of suddenly becoming more dependent on my husband by needing rides when my bus or commuter train was not in service.

But I was determined to buy, and so I said I could live with a nonsubway transportation option. This was supposed to suddenly open up a universe of fabulous new options, but, as we were annoyed to discover, we still had no truly good prospects. On a bus line, we saw a tiny one-bed whose big selling point was a two-by-four-foot "deck" padded with rubber. We bid on it—and lost. Then we found a bigger condo on a commuter rail line; that gem needed its roof replaced and was unhappily located directly across from a busy gas station. We bid on it anyway. And lost that too. To our embarrassment, it was becoming clear that we couldn't even afford to buy *bad* places.

My resolve wavering, I wondered aloud whether it might just be better to stay in our apartment instead of talking ourselves into buying a dump. I tried to position this option as a good thing by reminding Jason that we loved our neighborhood, and that waiting a year would let us approach the whole thing with more resources. Jason was not fooled by my positive spin.

We eventually agreed that if we didn't find anything before the last weekend of August, the last days of his vacation, we were going to bite the increased rent and stay put. Friday evening's showing: forgettable. Saturday's open houses: tragic. Sunday morning, I was up an hour before Jason, circling five open houses in five different places: Cambridge, Jamaica Plain, Brighton, Brookline, and—why not?—Malden. The first four locales are all part of the contiguous flow of Metro Boston, and each could meet one or both of my requirements. The last destination, Malden, I knew little of, except that it was the first or second North Shore town after it feels like you've left Boston. I circled the ad because it was a great deal and I was helpless at that point to resist anything in our price range that did not include the dreaded words "garden level" (i.e., below the snowline in a basement where the sun can't reach) or "as is" (one rotten floorboard shy of condemned).

When Jason got out of bed, he announced he was going to the beach. His love of lying out on the hot sand is matched only by the pleasure he takes in strolling about clad in a cocktail-napkin-sized bathing suit. My rigorous house-hunting regimen had denied him almost all opportunity to do both all summer, and now, on his last day before classes, he felt like he'd earned a little Bake and Shake It time. But I was horrified: I had a *plan*. I had been working on it for an hour, mapped out how to actually do all five open houses in all five places in the four hours the showings spanned. I couldn't possibly deviate from the *plan*.

Considering that all the other similarly well-planned days that summer had not paid off, Jason was not amused that I would, in a rare show of stubbornness, stick to my guns on this. I offered a truce: I suggested he go to the beach early and meet me at noon for the first open house. He said yes, but in that pinched way that really meant there were implied parenthetics involved. ("Yes, you bastard, I'll give up my last day before school—hell, maybe my last good day ever; maybe I'll be crippled tomorrow, and then won't you wish I'd gone to the beach? Not that I'm saying no, because, damn you, I'm saying yes.")

When he pulled up at the first open house—a two-room attic that had been billed as two bedrooms—he was a thunderclap on legs. As we drove away, he let me know that it had remained grey and miserable at the beach until the moment he set foot in the parking lot to leave. ("So, thanks a lot, Mister. Thanks a whole lot.") As we approached open house number two, we could see through the unit to the back parking lot; it was that shallow. ("ONE DAY. I just wanted ONE DAY.") Number three, in a basement, was a low-ceilinged warren which resembled a maze, through which dozens of low-end would-be homebuyers weaved and bobbed, trying to find their way out of the fluorescent hell and back into daylight. ("Oh yeah, *this* was worth the trip.")

Number four was the nadir of home-hunting. A rare "single home" advertised within our budget turned out to be an attached townhouse visibly listing to one side as we arrived. Another young couple was already there, and we walked up just as the husband said, "Would ya look at the crack in that foundation?" Not an auspicious start, but we trooped in to meet the Realtor, who pointed into a hole in the wall. Indicating the visible charring within, she cheerfully announced that there had been a fire in the basement the previous year but that everything—except, evidently, *the hole*—was all patched up now. When Jason, trying to be a sport, asked what was above the comically low dropped ceilings, the Realtor encouraged him to take a peek: unbelievably, six inches above was *another* dropped ceiling. As we quietly slipped away from the charred, cracking, forcibly shrunken "home," Jason said little. Even parenthetically, the car was ominously quiet.

As we found number five, the Malden place, we noticed one thing right away: green space. Malden is no bastion of nature, mind you, but this street was a condo complex comprised of brick townhouses organized along winding sidewalks, with green lawns, maple trees, and flowering shrubs between units. It only took one step through the door of that townhouse to know that leaving city limits had made all the difference. Though small, the place was ideal: a living room flowed into a dining room off a sunny kitchen. Upstairs, two bedrooms and a bathroom rounded out the 700 square feet. A door led to the shrub-enclosed backyard. Beyond that was the unit's assigned spot in the parking lot. And beyond that—could it be?—a pool.

All of this, delightful as it was, we passed without comment. We walked out to our car and drove away. Jason finally said aloud what we were both thinking, "The one nice place we've seen all summer and not a stupid train in sight." I'd have pointed out that there was no coffee shop either, but that would have been pushing it.

Sometimes, in a marriage, you may simply have to endure your partner's stony silence, knowing that the quiet is a passive-aggressive way of listing off your many shortcomings. You might choose, at these times, to engage and actually hear the list aloud. Or, fatigued, you may simply bite your tongue to keep from blurting out your own unhelpful, prerehearsed speeches about his attitude. I went the latter route when we got back to our soon-to-be very expensive apartment. At my desk, I busied myself with preparing for my own classes, while Jason . . . well, that's just it. I didn't know where Jason went. And I thought it best not to pad around after him immediately.

Eventually, the silence got to me and I cautiously peeked into the kitchen: no Jason. I walked down the hall, thinking he might be in the living room, trying to shake off the day with a nap. But no: the bathroom door was open, and there, sitting in the tub, sunk down to his neck, was my husband. It was quiet. And dark. I was unnerved. "What are you doing?" I asked.

If I'd been thinking, I would have been wise enough not to open myself up like that. He was ready—no, he was *waiting*—with an answer. He gave me a murderous look. "I'm pretending . . . I'm at . . . *the beach.*"

I thought about the Malden townhouse all night. It was just so clean and unstinky and above ground. For my money, those virtues made it a diamond after all, just in a very cheap setting. The next morning, without telling Jason, I decided I had not given Malden a chance. I called the Realtor and asked for a second look. That afternoon, I discovered that the subway—albeit the line I thought of as the least frequent—ran directly into Malden Center. With a map in hand, I found my way to the townhouse from the train. A twenty-minute walk, it wasn't a full mile away, but it hardly represented being close to public transportation for someone of my girth and temperament. As I walked down an unused industrial road and passed the nearby iron works, it was also clear to me that there was no coffee shop on my horizon if I decided I could live with this place.

And yet: when I turned onto our street—for that is what it would become—I heard the wind in the trees, like soft hands rubbing together, the sound rising and falling. It had never occurred to me that we could afford to hear anything other than emergency vehicles racing by or trucks backing up. I slipped into the backyard and sat on a bench in the sunlight, imagining how we would outline the lawn in tulips. I called Jason, who was just getting off work. "Come to Malden," I said. "We have a bid to make."

What was to follow was predictable in some ways: Lyra changed our interest rate and our closing costs at whim, which left us scrambling to cobble together several thousand more dollars at the last second. The last few days involved heated conversations and flaming faxes spitting out of machines at Lyra's bank, our lawyer's office, and the Realtor's office. It required a small loan from Jason's grandmother and each of us taking cash advances on our credit cards to pull it off, but we did it, and even had a few bucks left over to split a puu puu platter at the bad Chinese restaurant in our new neighborhood. (A month later, we would learn that Grampa Greenwood, who died earlier that year, had left us $10,000—which Jason's dad had not made liquid sooner, we suspect, in a kind of fiscal discipline lesson, so that we could prove that we were capable of buying on our own. Timing, apparently, is *not* everything.)

Four months after the day I found the landlord on my doorstep, we had no landlords but ourselves. I wasn't really close to a train, and the only coffee shop was a four-stool window-counter joint which served pump coffee with flavors like blueberry and cinnamon. Jason had no fireplace, but he did get parking, a yard, and plenty of cupboards. In some ways—profound ones—it was the biggest of my so-called compromises. But in other ways, it was also real progress: for the first time, we were homeowners, and now, more than ever, our fortunes were deeply aligned in a way that transcended rhetoric.

It was a classic trade-off: we achieved more independence from others at the cost of more dependence on each other. It's the kind of thing that can as easily strengthen a marriage as bust it down. But we didn't analyze the decision too much, for we felt as if we were finally growing up. Where house-hunting had seemed progressively to push us into opposing factions, owning a house put us back on the same team again. We reveled in planning what would come next: things like stripping the floors down to the natural wood, repainting the beige pink walls, and taking the romance-novel candelabra out of the shower. (*Honestly*. You can't make a detail like that up. Nor the fact that the bathroom was done in orange, purple, black, white, and brown.)

By late October, we were enjoying a better kind of silence than what we'd experienced on the final day of open houses. The day after we closed on the sale, we were in separate rooms upstairs in the townhouse, each painting the walls a new shade. Jason had wanted the bedroom to be soothing and restful, so he was busy painting it ice blue. I was in the study, warming it up with the golden color of the conservatory at my old college. We were working quietly, concentrating on finishing before the early setting sun would make it impossible to tell how the colors looked. We said little, only occasionally calling out questions to each other, without ever leaving our stations. Every now and then, I would hear Jason singing a snippet of a song, but I didn't comment because I didn't want to break the spell. I loved just hearing him there, knowing we had made it to this place. I felt so hopeful and proud of us: another folder closed, a new chapter opened, finally home.

9

Creature Comfort

THEY SAY THAT PEOPLE OFTEN LOOK LIKE THEIR PETS—OR
is it vice versa? Either way, while this may be true for platinum
blonde Maltese owners or gaunt runners who own grey-
hounds, the rule never applied to Jason and me when it came
to the few pets we owned in our years together. It most certainly didn't apply to the adorable little critter who shared our
new condo. I speak here of Poo, our house rabbit, whose presence made the domesticity of our home ownership complete.

For those not initiated into the odd lifestyle of lagomorph
husbandry—and I am guessing this would be most people—
"house rabbit" is the accepted term for a bunny bred and raised
for indoor living. Trained to use a litter box, sip from a water
bottle, and eat from a tray, these civilized creatures bear little resemblance to the only pet bunnies I ever saw when I was a child;
those rabbits were wooly, cowering beasts living in dark hutches
and just dying for the occasional backyard romp. House rabbits,
by contrast, live the good life, at liberty to wander about their

owners' homes, as unfettered as a free-range chicken but with no danger of eventually ending up a dinner special.

While it might be true, then, that Jason and I did not resemble our living slipper of a pet, it would be fair to assume that our choice of pet revealed something about us. What exactly that something was would become clear over the life span of our beloved Poo.

Poo's original name, given by the science department at the school where Jason worked, was Oreo, an obvious and unimaginative reflection of the bunny's coloring: black head and torso, with a white patch in between. But the children in Jason's classroom, where the rabbit was assigned, dubbed him with a name far less cliché, if even more stubbornly literal: Little Head. (Compared to his body, his head was in fact small, and there you have it.)

Little Head lived in a cage in the classroom and was only set free at Jason's discretion. Because rabbits are far more clever than you might think for creatures whose brains are the size of apricots, Little Head understood this dynamic and saw Jason as his great liberator. When released from his cage, instead of bolting for the cafeteria or even the playground, Little Head would stay close, running circles of delight around Jason's ankles.

On weekends, poor Little Head was left behind at school, kept company only by two days' worth of food and the empty desks of a darkened classroom. Jason, being tender of heart, hated this. But the rabbit was only on loan from the science department, so Jason could do nothing about this state of affairs. That all changed, though, when Jason's summer vacation came and the school asked him if he wanted to babysit Little Head until classes resumed in the fall.

This was supposed to be a temporary arrangement, but Jason loved having the bunny in our house. The bunny, free to roam around and eagerly hop onto furniture to see us, also seemed to enjoy the new arrangement. When classes began again, and Jason was supposed to return Little Head to the school, he balked. Now, Jason is an upstanding guy, so the idea of not returning the rabbit did not come easily for him. But it seemed cruel to him to recage the rabbit after so long. He couldn't bear it.

He could, I suppose, have passionately explained his feelings to the science department, but that isn't his nature. So instead he made up a ridiculous story: he said that while we were on vacation, we had let careless friends bunny-sit and those friends had let the bunny go by accident. It is a testament to the trusting spirit of the school official involved, or to her perception of Jason, that she accepted this story with grace and sympathetically asked if he would like a replacement bunny for his class. Jason politely declined.

Of course, before he did any of that, he asked me how I would feel about a bunny living in our midst permanently, which I had not signed on for when he brought the rabbit home. When he asked this, he looked as hopeful and happy as a kid talking his mom into letting him keep the puppy he found in the park. How could I say no?

To be honest, pet ownership had not previously been a high point of Jason's and my years together. He'd had more experience with pets as a child, including dogs, cats, and even a chicken named Fluff Machine (which may be the best pet name I have ever heard). I'd only had one real pet: Henrietta, a guinea pig whose brief time in my life was ended tragically when she was run over by a dump truck in front of my house.

Together, Jason and I had only one pet before Poo, and it hadn't gone very well.

Soon after we married, we decided we wanted a small dog. We couldn't have a cat because of Jason's allergies, and we couldn't have an Irish wolfhound or a Great Pyrenees because we lived in a small apartment. To do the right thing—and, okay, to save money—we went to the local chapter of the MSPCA to choose a dog from among the assorted strays. One immediately leapt out at us—literally. Zoe, an exotic looking blend of whippet and basenji, had been in the shelter for weeks already, after having been abandoned. Despite (or because of) her traumatic backstory, she kept enthusiastically jumping up into our view, with a clear "Love me! Love me!" expression. No other mutt in the place had anything approaching Zoe's personality, and so we brought her home. We bought her a fleece duckie, which she revered, and let her curl up on our chests for naps.

The problem with adopting a dog that has been abandoned is that she is likely to have abandonment issues—whenever we went out the door, Zoe was sure we were leaving her forever. What her doggy mind wanted was to be able to see us all the time, since the last time she took her eyes off an owner, she never saw that person again. Worse, we soon learned that being in a shelter for weeks can seriously screw with a dog's psychology; in Zoe's case, that meant she was both needy and aggressive in her own fashion. Even her breed was an issue: as a whippet mix, she needed to be able to run freely and at length, but we had only a crappy backyard off a busy city street to offer. Add the fact that both Jason and I were gone for hours a day, and things were doomed from the start. We simply hadn't realized what Zoe would need from us, and by the time we realized we couldn't provide it, things had gotten ugly.

Zoe became the Mistress of Displeasure. If I came home and played ball with her for a half hour, she was ecstatic—until I stopped to use the bathroom or sit my weary ass down for a moment. Then, the time I'd spent playing was completely forgotten, replaced by rage that I would dare think I could ignore her for a moment. Displeasure must be shown, and this would take the form of, say, peeing in my shoes. If one of us was petting her and then stopped to answer a ringing phone, she might well just give us a haughty look as she backed out of sight—to poop on the Oriental rug.

Within three weeks, we realized that we were no match for her. We couldn't stay at home to make her feel better; we didn't have enough open space for her to work out her nervous energy; and we just didn't know the first thing about reprogramming the canine version of *Carrie*. We both understood this, but approached it from slightly different angles: I was worried about my mental health and the quality of our daily lives; Jason was worried about Zoe's happiness and didn't want us to make a hard life even harder. Swallowing hard, we gave Zoe to a man who lived in the country and whose wife was looking for a dog to keep her company at home all day. It was clearly a better fit for Zoe, but even as we handed over her fleece duckie, we berated ourselves for failing. Silly as it may sound, we wondered whether we would ever make decent parents if we couldn't keep a dog around for a month.

Past history, then, was not the best guide for how bunny ownership would go. But Jason pointed out some significant differences between our new pet and our old one: the bunny did not need constant companionship and, indeed, living with us would vastly increase his human interaction; as far as we knew, the bunny had demonstrated no psychotic tendencies; and our tiny condo would seem an expansive paradise for the little beast, compared to either cage or classroom. Best of all, house rabbits are fairly low maintenance: you just feed them, clean up their messes, and let them hop around—end of story.

It sounded like the best possible way to ease back into pet ownership and maybe even prove that we could take care of a being other than ourselves. And, really, Jason's description of how easy life with a bunny had been in the classroom was pretty much on the money. The only detail that had been underplayed was the issue of poop. Bunnies poop. *A lot.* It's one of the things they do best, and our bunny was a champion, which is how Little Head became Poo. Though house rabbits like ours can be trained to use a litter box, nothing guarantees how precise they will be.

We also soon learned that Poo was afraid of the first floor. That is, he was afraid of getting to it from the second floor. Due to his own bunny physiology, he found our stairs quite difficult to manage and never attempted to descend or climb them on his own. We brought him to the first floor for a good hop one evening, and he paused long enough to sniff out what direction he'd come from before hopping over to the stairs to return. Perhaps the stairs were too shallow or too slippery, as his progress was slow and labored; yet he continued upward, until he was about three-quarters of the way to the top, where he froze. He hunkered down and tensed up, remaining perfectly still, as if he were a soldier in a foxhole awaiting fire.

Watching this, we were puzzled. Why give up so close to his goal? Climbing the stairs behind him, we saw the answer: the cool Scandinavian mobile we had hung in the stairwell was casting rotating shadows over the rabbit. The poor thing had been almost home free when he saw the circling shadow and, despite not having ever experienced the wild himself, instinctively panicked. In his very small mind, the dark shapes bobbing on air above him must be the predators that his species naturally feared. Raised indoors, he can be forgiven for not knowing that neither hawks nor owls are made from brightly colored plastic discs. Misguided or not, now that he believed that the stairs were a dangerous realm, he refused to go anywhere near them ever again.

Our top-floor life with Poo was much happier than our experience with Zoe. We discovered how ridiculously social a rabbit can be, taking great pleasure in hanging out wherever we were, as well as how mischievous, waiting for the perfect opportunity to snack on a broom left unprotected or shredding a bill that had fallen to the floor. Each morning, he guarded the shower as we bathed, sitting like a sentinel on the bath mat until we finished and then hopping away. During the afternoon, Poo liked to sit immobile in an available patch of sunlight, or nap under a dresser or nightstand (where no owls could reach). But come evening, he wanted to play a round or two of tag—racing up to Jason's foot and then racing away, not too far, so Jason could follow. At bedtime, the rabbit would hop around to Jason's side of the bed and thump to get his attention, so that Jason would bring him up for some cuddle time while reading before going to sleep.

You'll notice that Poo predominantly directed his attention at Jason. I was a decent substitute if Jason was unavailable, but Poo's preference was clear. Was it because Jason, like the bunny, was furry, and thus seemed a more kindred species?

Or was it because Jason was still imprinted on the rabbit as savior from the school? I suspect the answer is more simple: Poo knew who loved him best.

Yes, I liked our bunny and enjoyed the uniqueness of our pet in a cat-and-dog world. But Jason showered affection on the little bun, and there was no mistaking that he meant it. I've heard before that how a man treats his mother is a good indication of what kind of husband he'll be; I'd suggest looking at how he treats animals. Only personal ethics requires you to treat animals with the kindness typically reserved for humans, and the only rewards are personal. That Jason could be so loving to a creature whose expression never changed revealed a gentleness and a sweetness that he typically masked with the cynical wit and jaded affect of a sophisticated urban thirty-something.

But just how much Jason loved the Poo didn't become clear until we were preparing for a weekend trip to Montreal. Typically, Jason gets so excited about a return to his old stomping grounds (having attended college at McGill University) that he can think of little else in the week beforehand. The shopping, the food, the dancing—these had always been the topics that led up to Montreal trips in times past. But once we had the bunny, Jason worried about how it would fare in our absence. Granted, this was an animal that had lived for years without any companionship on weekends, so it was in no danger of real trauma; but we both agreed that we wanted a friend to come in and check on the bunny each day and make sure it didn't feel too forlorn. Jason, however, worried that this would not be enough. Enter bunny cam.

Jason, only half jokingly, hit upon the concept of taking the tiny webcam attached to our computer and directing it at the rabbit's cage, so we could then theoretically observe how the wee thing fared over the weekend. This would not be easy, not least of all because our enormous caveman-era desktop was not in the same room as the bunny and would have to be moved for the weekend. Beyond that remained the question of where the camera could send the image. Were we going to open a chat session on the web and hope it remained open the entire time we were in Montreal? And, if we did that, would we really pause from our shopping-eating-dancing whirlwind in hopes of seeing an image of the bunny? We never did create bunny cam, but all that weekend, Jason bemoaned this fact.

A weekend trip away only scratched the surface of our feelings for Poo. Rabbits are prone to a variety of diseases, mostly intestinal, which often kill those poor field bunnies who have no indulgent benefactors. One day that first fall we lived in the condo, Jason said he was sure that Poo seemed unlike himself; I was sure that my husband was overreacting. I mean, it's not like the look on the bunny's face was suddenly pained or anything, and even a bunny must have the occasional off day, right? But Jason knew better. When the bunny wouldn't play tag before bedtime that night and didn't guard us in the shower in the morning, it was clear something was up. At mealtime, he didn't run for his food but retreated as far as possible under our bed, a bad sign.

We packed him off to Angell Memorial Hospital, the nearest emergency veterinary center, a surreal world where a Saint Bernard might have surgery down the hall from a python getting an X-ray. The doctor on call examined Poo, and she told us that he'd have to be hospitalized for two or three days, needing an IV drip and several rounds of medications to deal with an intestinal blockage that could kill him. She asked us if we wanted to go through with this or not. For a moment, I think we didn't understand the question. She was asking whether we wanted to pay for treatment, which was not going to be cheap.

Not cheap translated to nearly a thousand dollars. In bunny care. We didn't even have a thousand dollars liquid between us at that moment. To be honest, we both had moments of hesitation over the four-figure bill. But this was our bunny, whom we had come to love. Maxing out a credit card, we signed an agreement to pay for treatment and trusted that they would send us back a healthy bunny for our trouble. And when he was home hopping around our feet, albeit with a tiny little IV prick visible in his fur, it did seem worth it.

Some of our friends could hardly believe we'd spent nearly a thousand bucks on a pet we essentially stole (which is a harsh but accurate way to describe the liberation of Poo). And in general, many of our friends seemed to find our devotion to our odd little pet amusing. It was hard to convince people that we weren't making it up when we said our bunny played games or liked to groom Jason's arms with his little tongue. This skepticism was understandable because whenever friends came for dinner, Poo was upstairs away from the action, so they didn't see his personality on display. And he didn't always bother to seek out those guests who made it to the second floor. People would peer into our bedroom and see him sitting still as a stone on an area rug, and more than once guests assumed he was a stuffed animal.

We would only have Poo for a few years, as he would later succumb to one of those bunny illnesses. But in the time we

had him, he came to be a defining part of our lives. Yes, owning a rabbit was rare—no one else we knew did—but the Poo
was still just a pet, after all, not an alien life form. He had the
same basic needs as our friends' cats and dogs and provided a
similar amount of joy and companionship. In many ways, it
was as if we had picked out the pet that most resembled our
marriage: far more exotic in principle than in practice, and the
perfect fit for us. In fact, though he may not have borne a
physical resemblance to either Jason or me, you could say he
looked a lot like the two of us after all.

A Threat to Marriage?

10

~

Go Toward
What You Love

AT THIRTY-FOUR, IT FINALLY FELT LIKE EVERYTHING HAD come together: a good marriage, a decent home (complete with adorable pet), a new job that I loved at Tufts University, and a great community of friends. Every weekend, we'd invite people over to dinner, gathering around our dining-room table in cold weather and surrounding a rickety picnic table in the backyard on warm nights. Our lives simply couldn't have been more domestic if we'd tried.

In a movie, any scene of easy bliss is sure to presage some terrible threat. Considering what a film buff I am, perhaps I should have been on alert for signs of danger. And when I look back now, it's hard to believe that I hadn't noticed we were headed for trouble. After years of faulty compromises and a near-total aversion to serious discussion of contentious subjects, Jason and I hadn't developed any skills for handling the parts of our interior lives that didn't nicely align. While some people spend all their time looking for hints of trouble in their romantic relationships, even imagining phantom problems, I had never looked at all. And by the time I did search my memory for the first fissure in our union, I came up with a thousand seemingly innocent examples of moments when we'd chosen the easy way out of a potential tussle, setting up instead the Mother of All Conflicts to come.

Thanksgiving Day 2001, nearly seven years after we married, was the formal beginning of the great slide downward. I say "formal beginning" because I finally had to acknowledge that already things were not as perfect as I had imagined. I did not want to face this; just as I could have been convinced to rent the shrink-wrapped apartment for years because of my desire to avoid change, I would've been perfectly content to keep our marriage just trucking along as it always had. My husband, it turns out, didn't feel this way—not that he told me. Therein lies the problem.

Jason and I were driving back from Thanksgiving at his mom's house in New Hampshire, where we'd spent the afternoon with his family. That day, everyone had been in fine spirits, except that by the end of the meal Jason was making what I thought were snarky little comments. I can't even recall what about, other than that each barb served to poke at me in some fashion. Once we were in the car, I asked what was up. He shrugged, said, "Nothing," and kept his eyes on the road.

I didn't push it. This was a dynamic that had begun to haunt us: he'd hold something against me but not tell me, and I'd convince myself that if it really mattered, he'd say so. Sometimes, if this went on for days, I might give in and try to speak *for* him—trying to guess what the issue was—and let him confirm or deny my summary. And while I knew that Thanksgiving Day that something was up, I didn't want to wade into some huge mess—which, intuitively, I knew it would be—during a season when I would be trying to grade the semester's final essays, get our holiday shopping done, and get ready for our annual Solstice party.

This party, named ecumenically so as to celebrate all things warm and wonderful without insulting anyone's deities, had been our favorite tradition for years. Forty or fifty people would crowd into whatever too-small place we lived in at the time, eating Jason's baked goods, drinking cocktails, and making all kinds of merry.

That Solstice, our closest friends raised their glasses as we lit candles and offered our usual toast to those who were there with us, those who could not be there, and to all our future Solstices to come. To the assembled guests, as we would often hear later, we looked like we ever did: happy and in love, the VGs (as we were known) throwing a party. We didn't appear to be two people studiously avoiding any real discussion on the eve of their seventh wedding anniversary. It was a little like Oscar Wilde's barbed tale *The Picture of Dorian Gray*, in which a vain young man trades his soul in order to keep his good looks for decades, while a portrait of him ages horribly in an attic. Had Wilde, keen observer, been at our Solstice party, he might well have wondered whether there was a painting of us melting somewhere upstairs.

In retrospect, it's a little galling to think that we were felled by the seven-year itch. No one wants to be a cliché, but right on cue (at least if you use our wedding anniversary as a yardstick), we were floundering. Once the holidays were past, I again asked

Jason whether something was up. He didn't answer at first, and in many ways, he couldn't have, at least not with any accuracy. It would be many months before the real issue came to light—a kind of early midlife crisis for Jason that involved a complete reexamination of who he saw himself to be—and he didn't yet have any way to say what he was really feeling. Instead, he did what we all do when confronted by something we're not yet ready to face—he deflected. He chose an easy target, one that was sure to hold my attention: my weight.

I had gained almost fifty pounds since we married. In context, I should point out that Jason had met and married me at my lowest adult weight, soon after I had lost 130 pounds. So while it should have shamed me to have put on so much weight again, I was still kind of proud of having actually kept off eighty of the pounds I'd lost in the first place. You can debate the merits of that logic all day long, but the fact of the matter is that Jason—who considers a pair of size thirty-two Levis his fat jeans—found himself married to a bigger guy than the one who had once forgotten his (much smaller) wedding pants.

Now, the lard was on the table. I could hardly pretend otherwise, but I at least wanted to know what was prompting the discussion at that particular moment; in reply, he nervously mumbled that a relative had started talking about my weight. How did I think that made him feel? It *embarrassed* him. Nervously, I asked him what this all meant. He didn't have an answer. So, in an approach I would recommend to absolutely no one, I answered for him, saying it sounded like maybe he was regretting marrying me. Maybe he felt like he had settled for something he shouldn't have. Note how I went right to the most horrible reading of the issue; this is the flip side of being a big schmaltzball: in arguments, it's all drama, all the time.

I have a tendency to do something our friend Deb calls "awfulizing": I imagine the worst-case scenario for every event. For instance, if I love you, I have imagined you dead in countless terrible and tragic ways. I think this is my preemptive way of ensuring that I can survive the worst, having practiced it so many times. And that night, I awfulized what would happen next, envisioning Jason leaving his fat husband and hooking up with some slender young guy who, I was righteously sure, would never be able to replicate what we had, slim hips or not.

It was only a few weeks later that Jason and I were supposed to go on a trip to Vegas, which we had planned with the specific intention of spending hours poolside as an escape from the New England winter. But the last thing I wanted to do was go anywhere that put my newly chastised body on display in a swimsuit. That prospect was only marginally worse than thinking of being in a buffet line with Jason watching me fill my plate. The actual trip could have only been a more nerve-wracking enterprise if we'd agreed to film it for reality television. Strenuously trying to maintain enthusiasm for our vacation, I felt we had a kinship with the performers in Cirque du Soleil: you've never seen people working so hard to act like they're having an effortless time.

Over the following months, Jason and I kept mum about our troubles. We continued to invite friends over for dinner and kept seeing our families, none of whom knew about the painting in the attic. But when we were alone, we took to spending a lot of our free time on separate floors of the house. Remaining technically faithful, we nonetheless discovered there are many ways monogamists can cheat.

For me, it came in the form of an intense friendship with Harry, the neighbor who lived across the yard from us. In a few short months, he'd become an extended part of the household, often coming to eat supper with us and join us on outings. While he was a friend that we made as a couple, Harry and I naturally gravitated toward each other because of a shared interest in movies and music. Suddenly, I had someone to talk with about the trippy new Bulgarian movie or the latest Le Tigre CD.

In a coincidence that could be seen as either well- or ill-timed, just as things started to cool between Jason and me, Harry showed up on our doorstep to ask if I wanted to go with him while he walked his dog, Elvis. Jason and I were communicating tensely at this point, so I leapt at the chance for some easy conversation. What I said to Jason, however, was that it would be good exercise for me. He could hardly argue, all things considered, and after that first night, the walk became a routine.

Underneath, though, there was more to it than a change of pace: just when I was feeling least appealing as a person, someone had chosen me to be his friend. But the effect on Jason was just as profound: he felt as if he'd been passed over, like the person not picked for the team. For so long, whoever we met as a couple had remained a friend of the couple, and this shift to a seemingly unequal personal friendship hurt him.

I didn't want to admit this, because my daily life often felt so solitary. Because of my itinerant teacher lifestyle, I had always taught my classes and then left the campus immediately, maintaining no office, serving on no committees, and spending the rest of my time writing. I didn't have coworkers with whom I could casually chat every day, and most of my friends had become *our* friends, people I saw at dinner parties. Many days, outside of my classroom lectures, I interacted with no one at all but Jason. Into this came a real friendship which offered daily contact—a dog must be walked, after all—and I couldn't pass it up.

I'd like to say that I never realized the rebuke Jason felt from the blossoming of this connection just as our own faltered. But as Harry and I started going to movies and concerts together, I knew in my heart how much this bothered Jason, how it transferred some of my isolation onto him. Even so, I put up a defensive wall, telling myself that if he wanted to join me in these pursuits, he could do so—not that I asked anymore.

What happened next? The more time I spent with Harry, the colder Jason became. The colder Jason became, the more time I spent with Harry, pouring my heart out. Harry and I eventually developed the shared language a close friendship engenders, with inside jokes, catch phrases, and a mutual understanding often expressed in a raised eyebrow or a smile from across the table. I reveled in the intimacy of it.

Imagine, then, being Jason: his husband was spending all this time, energy, and spirit on building a relationship with another man. No matter that the guy was straight and perpetually checking out the local ladies; no one since Jason has taken up so much of his husband's time. Jason finally couldn't stand keeping quiet about it. "You act like he's your boyfriend," he said to me on a rare night when we were sitting together on our sofa, like the couple we had once been.

I didn't deny it. I knew what he meant: lack of physical chemistry notwithstanding, I had devoted as much time to nurturing this friendship as to beginning a romantic relationship, and the whole thing had an intensity that was nearly inexplicable. I said I understood what Jason was feeling but I needed the friendship anyway. And then, partly because I couldn't leave the focus on me and partly just because it was true, I said, "If you spent less time upstairs, maybe we'd spend more time together."

"Upstairs" was a not-especially-subtle euphemism for Jason's own version of straying: alone in our second-floor study, he was taking his walks on the wild side on the Internet. Around the time he'd begun making his snide remarks the previous fall, I'd noticed that the history file in our Web browser was getting erased every time he was on the computer. This was the first time in our married lives that I had felt overtly excluded from what he was thinking or doing. Our openness about whom and what we found attractive had suddenly disappeared. If he was erasing his steps after all this time, what wasn't I supposed to see?

When I finally did stumble onto one of the sites usually erased, I was chagrined to discover that it wasn't very reflective of my sexual tastes or, up to that point, as far as I knew, of my husband's. Jason was a little red-faced when I asked him about it, but he assured me it was just harmless fun, no threat to our relationship.

Trying to be all adult and what progressives call "sex positive," I said that as long as this new fascination was limited to the Web, I could deal with it. I even went online myself for a period, looking to see if there existed any place where a man like me would be the thing that was desired, as I was not desired at home. I found a Web site specifically celebrating Chubs, as plus-sized gay men were delicately called, and Chasers, the men who loved them. (The Web, it is clear, has an inexhaustible capacity for fostering the niche-iest of niches.) This site and its users embraced me, which was initially so exciting I even told Jason about it. But then it began to worry me. The boundaries seemed porous; it appeared too easy to get lured into the possibility of outside activity if I formed attachments on the Web. And why spend time forging cyber connections when my live one was in such unsteady shape? Chatting just because my husband did and then calling it openness was as reactive and useless as capitulating and calling it compromise. I decided to let the Web world spin without me and told Jason so.

As that summer approached, then, we were at cross purposes. Jason couldn't resist the lure of the chat room, which struck me as risky, not to mention a huge time drain. But then again, I was spending my hours with Harry without inviting Jason. We were on a roller coaster: some nights we would cuddle up and promise to solve things; other nights, we could barely finish dinner together.

That summer, we went "therapist shopping," by which I mean we did sessions at three different therapists before settling on the third. The first therapist, to Jason's growing panic, announced that we'd do fun games like pretending to be each other's parents; clearly, this was a woman without in-laws of her own, or she would have recognized the absurdly high risk in such "fun." Later, another therapist charged $180 an hour and then made up important-sounding bogus words like "distillization," as if we were paying him by the syllable. A third therapist, Big Eyes, seemed just right: a concerned-looking gay man who dealt with lots of couples in crisis.

Unfortunately for us, Big Eyes operated like this: first, he'd ask what happened that week. We would give impossibly conflicting answers. Then he'd look sad. Then he'd ask me what I felt Jason was saying. I'd start awfulizing and say I was sure Jason meant something really horrible. Then, instead of asking Jason whether this was an overstatement or an accurate reading of his feelings, Big Eyes would let it pass for truth, while looking *really* sad. And time would be up. All this trained professional ever managed to do was replicate our pattern from home where Jason didn't say what he was really feeling and I filled in the blanks with only quasi-accurate language.

Meanwhile, we were transforming. I lost thirty pounds that summer, through a combination of obsessive power-walking and being so stressed out that I could barely keep food in my system. The pounds fell off fast enough that my nutritionist gently suggested I might slow down. I was determined to stake out my own identity: growing my hair out and dressing in thrift-store finds that better suited the rock shows I was going to. I got a lot of praise from people—everyone loves to see fat folk lose weight, even rapidly—and I was feeling pretty good about my rejuvenated self. And it seemed to revive Jason as well: he shaved his head, picked up a short leather jacket he looked sexy in, and started wearing boot-cut jeans, very butch. We had, in a brief period of time, gone from being two guys with short haircuts and similar swingers-era shirts to two men each with his own aesthetic—as we should have had all along.

I found this the only hopeful sort of progress that summer—at least I did until one night at dinner when Jason referred to my new look as my "midlife crisis." The comment pissed me off: after digging at my appearance for months, now he minded that I was trying to look good? When I complained about this to my ever-perceptive friend Amy, she said, "Ah ha!" sounding like a good detective. "His subconscious got the words out, but the midlife crisis is his, not yours. You're just in the way." There was a ring of truth to this; there were things in Jason's life he wasn't getting from our relationship, but neither of us had a clue how to deal with that.

Big Eyes was not a big help. As fall approached, it got to a point where Jason and I might arrive at therapy together, but we would inevitably go home our separate ways. Somehow our therapist could spoil any fragile truce, souring the air between us. We spent less and less time in the house together and, when we were together, icy silences prevailed.

We wanted things from each other that we once assumed were implied by our wedding vows but, in fact, simply couldn't be given: Jason wanted the sunlight from me to shine only on him again, while I wanted assurances that he was committed to me no matter what I looked like. Both of these desires lacked balance and were perhaps subconsciously designed to be un-meetable: if we couldn't have our all-or-nothing requests met, we could safely blame the other when things fell apart. And that was the scary thing—we were each beginning to imagine that maybe life would be easier if it didn't work out after all.

We'd gotten to a point where we spent our days circling around each other in near total silence. We were having meals together much less often, and we spent the evenings on separate floors—if I stayed home at all instead of going out to the movies or spending time with Harry. At night, Jason and I dutifully crawled into bed together but rolled away from each other. I could barely eat at this point (great for the diet!) and found myself constantly bursting into tears. This happened even on public transportation, which is a terrible place to sob, exposed as I was to your typical jaded Bostonian, whose first instinct will be "Don't look at the nut job . . . ," followed by, "Oooh, *look* at the nut job!"

I remember one late summer afternoon in particular when, on my bus ride home, I couldn't stop crying. My tears set off a Vietnamese lady, who bent double weeping over her bag of cans, and then an elderly Haitian gentleman who gave me a reproachful look as he wiped his eyes and got off the bus. I gulped in air but couldn't stop—which was deeply mortifying.

Something had to change.

That night, I told Jason that I thought I should move out. If there was any chance of repairing us, I would need to repair myself first. And as long as we continued to fill the house with emotional poison, I couldn't see us making it. He told me he understood and sadly said that he wouldn't fight me on this. His response, which seemed kind, was a huge relief to me, but as I would later find out, inside he was actually seething, believing that no matter what I called it, I was leaving him.

In the next few weeks, I tried to keep busy with the details of the move. On Craig's List, I found a dim and not especially clean room in an apartment shared by two guys fresh out of college. This was not exactly a leap forward in adult living, but I was desperate, so I signed on for it. Incredibly, Jason and I continued to have friends over for dinner, including the very night before my move. Dorian Gray to the end, we sat in our backyard together, knowing it might be the last time, watching the sparks from the grill light up the darkness, and never hinted that we were anything but a happy couple.

The morning I was to move out, I tried to put the best face on things, as if it was just a mutual decision that would be good for us. It was a show-stopping act of denial, and I kept it up through breakfast, until Jason finally started shouting at me that I had forced this on him, that he couldn't believe I was doing this. A good therapist might have been able to point out that the rare screaming on Jason's part was an indicator of the depths of his feelings; but we had fired Big Eyes and so no longer had a therapist, good or otherwise. What we had were wounded hearts, and I was more sure than ever that my moving out would be the right thing to do.

Later that morning, while Jason was at work, I finished packing up my things. As I came down the stairs with the last bag, I opened the front door and then stopped. There, on the coat hook, was Jason's leather jacket. I took it in both hands, buried my face in it, and wept. And then went out the door, leaving it behind.

Just as I hadn't been able to see what would lead to our breakup, I couldn't possibly have predicted what would begin the path to reconciliation. Three months later, I was forced to move back in with Jason—and not because I wanted to. While I was away for a weekend in New York, my roommates had decided to rent out my share of the hovel. I had to be out by December 1, just a few days away. This did not strike me as a happy turn of events.

A major source of my anxiety was that, in the months since I'd moved out, Jason had been working on exploring the parts of his life he felt he'd missed out on by settling down so early. He had been thinking about seriously checking out the "leather" scene, a subculture in the gay community. This was going to be a problem, I thought; the leather scene is pretty butch—all boots and uniforms—and I just don't have butch in me. But then Jason made it clear he wasn't asking any such thing of me. He said that he'd finally realized that most of the recent difficulties in our relationship had been about him figuring out what he wanted, not for us but for himself. He wasn't asking me to join him in his exploits; he was announcing to me the new life he was going to make *on his own*. I could have kicked myself. After all, I was the one who had packed my bags and walked out the door; I could hardly be surprised that the man I left behind would find his own way to move on.

After that conversation, I grew convinced that he was over our marriage entirely and that he was glad to be free. I didn't yet know that he often cried so much on the way to work in the morning that his coworkers had begun to worry about him. They were seeing him wrestling terribly with the pain of our break-up, while I went about my days sure that he was thrilled with the prospect of a new life.

Despite the complicated emotional terrain, Jason found my move home to be eminently practical: it would save money (no more would I be paying rent on top of the mortgage, which we still shared), and we could find our new direction—as friends? as something more?—together in our own home. I was skeptical about this, yet had no choice but to inflate my air mattress in our catch-all spare room anyway, settling into the strange arrangement. We set new ground rules for things: unless or until we got back together, we could see other people, but those relations were to be kept private and out of our home. It was all very adult-sounding, if not exactly progress toward reunion.

One weekend, Jason went to Montreal, well-known for its gay club scene, to check out the bars, and I made a date with an Italian hunk who liked big guys like me. But these brief forays into life outside our marriage were pretty weak. In Montreal, Jason didn't speak to a single guy, staying quietly to the side of the action. On my date, when I could get a word in edgewise with the smirking lothario, I spent most of my time talking about Jason.

As Christmas approached, Jason was beginning to think that maybe he didn't need to give up our marriage to find his new self. He wanted to remain faithful to me and make our union work. True to form, he didn't say this, and so I was still primed to think the worst one afternoon when the phone rang. It was a man's voice on the line, and he started talking to me as if we knew each other. Before I could figure out who he was, he asked if Dave was around, checking out whether it would be okay to talk. I told him I was Dave and asked if he wanted my husband. Remarkably, instead of doing what I would've done in his shoes—shriek and hang up—he said yes. And so I had the bitter task of calling my husband to the phone to chat up a stranger in my presence. I took this as my cue that we needed to officially end things.

On December 23, I told Jason I was done. I loved him but I was convinced that he had, ultimately, gotten me to do for him what he could not do for himself: break us up so he could be free. As ever, I had overshot the actual state of things by a mile. That's when my pragmatic scorner of emotion did something I never expected. He cried. And cried and cried. Honestly, he kind of howled. I was so thrown by this display of emotion that I bawled too. He begged me not to give up, or at least to go back into therapy so we could break up better and still have something left. Feeling stubbornly distrustful, I said no.

In the morning, he flew off to his family in Michigan without me, but not before pleading with me to reconsider. "At least come out for Christmas," he said. "You're my *family*." This was absurdly touching to me, but I didn't make any promises. Even so, the lure of Christmas in Michigan was powerful. I hadn't been away from Jason on Christmas in nine years at that point. And there is nowhere on earth I enjoy Christmas more than at Linda and Jim's. Their crowded Christmas Eve party is the liveliest, cheeriest swarm of humanity imaginable, followed the next morning by the calm of a quiet family-only Christmas. When Linda got on the phone later that day and told me I should still come, and Jason said he thought so too, I packed my bags and headed off, despite feeling as if it was a little insane to show up at the home of my in-laws immediately after dumping their son.

Christmas Eve.

The last of the fifty guests had long gone. Linda had dispatched Jason's little sister to bed. Jim had retired for the night, with Jason following soon after. But Linda had kept me busy picking up plates of cookies and empty glasses. Even as I was rubbing my eyes, she asked me to stay up a little longer, to put on my pajamas and come visit with her awhile.

We had just settled in for a chat, each of us ensconced on a couch in front of the Christmas tree, when she looked me in the eye and asked, "Is this your last Christmas with us, Dave?"

I started to cry. I didn't know the answer. But Linda wasn't going to leave it there. I found myself recounting the events of the past year, starting with the hurt of the comments about my weight. "But your weight's not about him," she said. When I tried to explain, she asked, "Why do you care so much what he thinks about it? You're the one who has to be happy with yourself." I moved on to the tension around my friendships and

Jason's jealousy. "Tell him to go make friends of his own, then," she said. I pointed out that he already had friends, and she shrugged, "So then it's no problem." I finally raised the specter of Jason needing a new lifestyle, and she asked something that floored me. "If he's the one who needs a new life, why are you the one breaking up?" Good question.

We talked for several hours, Linda returning again and again to two questions: Did I love Jason? Yes. What did I really want? For us to be happy again. If those answers were true, then what was I doing ending things? What sense did it make for me to break up because of what I imagined Jason wanted? At the heart of the matter, she said, I ought to be thinking about what *I* wanted and how to get there. She didn't use these exact words, but this is the message I heard: go toward what you love.

Years before, I'd heard a sermon about hope. The young minister, a new seminary grad, explained that she believed hope was not about the results but the process. Being hopeful, she explained, was recognizing one's desire for something, not merely fearing the loss of that thing. Knowing what you want is an illuminating force, one that spurs you forward to do whatever you can to move closer to that which would give you joy. Hope, then, is the attitude as you act upon your best impulses, and in itself it betters the quality of your life along the way. If the outcome is not what was hoped for, the loss doesn't erase how the hopefulness improved the journey.

If I really wanted to have my marriage back and our love restored, could I do any less hopeful thing than throw in the towel, ostensibly on my husband's behalf, even after he had made it clear he didn't want me to give up? Perhaps that would have made more sense if I believed in my heart that I didn't love him anymore, or that I couldn't see my life twined with his in the future. But the truth was that, complicated as things were and would be, I could still see us sharing our lives. When I thought of that possibility, I could hardly speak because I wanted it so much.

It was hard to accept the truth: the universe did not promise me anything. I was tiny and it was vast, and it had no intention of slowing the spin of its galaxies to solve my problems for me. It was up to me, then, to put hope in motion by going toward what I loved. And, yes, that was still Jason.

Linda finally rose from the couch and I followed suit. She clicked off the lamps, while I kept my counsel, not ready to say I was going to give things one more try. But I hugged her as we headed to bed.

"Look, Dave," she whispered, pointing out the front window into the dark.

As we'd chatted, a thick blanket of snow had transformed the neighborhood into a postcard scene. Fat snowflakes swirled downward, lit only by the streetlamp, and it was magical. Like a sign, the snow echoed the night of the long-ago Tuck & Patti concert, when Jason had first kissed my forehead. That night had been a beginning for us, a shift in our relationship that led us forward to the next level. Maybe, I thought, this night could lead us too.

11

How the Other Half Proposes

TYPICALLY, IF A PERSON DECIDES TO STICK WITH HIS marriage, he doesn't also have to consider whether or not to tie the knot. Most people either are married or they're not, and, naively, a fair number think that walking down the aisle ends the subject of whether you want to spend your life with someone. But Jason and I are gay people, which is just like being citizens except for minor details like equal rights. So, while our marriage may have been widely accepted in certain circles, it had never been legal before. But then the possibility of actual same-sex marriage arose, and we found ourselves with a new forum for testing what commitment meant and whether legal matrimony had anything to do with it.

Legal same-sex marriages were to begin in Massachusetts in May 2004. This was the outgrowth of a case which had spent several years in the state's court system, capped by a

Massachusetts Supreme Judicial Court ruling in late 2003 that said gays must be allowed to marry. Halfway through the six-month period that the justices allowed between their ruling and the first nuptials, Jason and I finished a year of couple's counseling with the kind of therapist who gives the industry a good name. Liz, the therapist, never made us do impressions of family members, and she only used words that actually appear in a dictionary; more important, she managed to see through every argument, accusation, and complaint to what was underneath: concern about our relationship.

We'd started seeing her just a few weeks after that crucial Christmas Eve, and in the ensuing year we had bounced back remarkably. Liz helped us grow comfortable with each other physically, accepting that intimacy comes in a variety of ways and that, in the bedroom like anywhere else, difference can merely be difference. She also helped us find a better balance between building our relationship and maintaining our distinct identities. Our return to a happy union made us missionaries for marital counseling. The first time I passed Liz's number on to friends, it felt empowering. It was a little like when an evangelical missionary hands a lost soul a pamphlet, or when a goodhearted stoner gets to share an especially sweet blend: the high of dispensing something sure to make the recipient feel much, much better.

Our openness about this topic was quite a change from the days when we'd maintained our model couple façade even while I was packing my bags. Sounding a bit like confirmed alcoholics—step one: admit you have a problem—we now kept our friends abreast of our struggle. To our surprise, of the couples we knew who'd been together as long as we had, almost every one had already ended up in therapy. Mention the topic at

a dinner party and a stream of stories would begin: bad therapists, crazy therapists, and even a few of the rare Liz-quality
ones. Like pashmina in the nineties, or Ugg boots ten years
later, couple's counseling was a true must-have. Who'd have
ever guessed that therapy was the new black?

It was during this era of renewed confidence that gay marriage
became a real possibility. You might think that Jason and I—as
a couple who'd already had a wedding, survived a painful separation, and recently celebrated their ninth anniversary—would
be ideal candidates for marriage. Certainly our friends and family thought so. Nearly from the moment that the Supreme Judicial Court had scheduled the May deadline for gay marriage,
we'd been getting phone calls asking when we would make it
legal. People can be forgiven for this assumption not only because we had so often talked about doing so, but because every
time the legislature met to debate the topic, we were out on the
steps of the Capitol loudly shouting down the antigay protes-
tors, some bused in from as far away as Georgia. Nonetheless,
talk of legal marriage became the first big challenge to our
newly repaired union.

My first instinct, upon the court's initial ruling, was to be
thrilled. But almost immediately, to my surprise, I felt skeptical,
too. When gay couples in a celebration at the Old South Meeting Hall began chanting "No more second-class citizens!" I
wanted to be unabashedly enthusiastic, but I also wondered if
the second class had just been shunted onto new people: single
people or people in nontraditional relationships who preferred
not to marry. Instead of actually guaranteeing equality, this ruling merely broadened which groups were included. That was a
lofty goal in itself, to be sure, but at the same time it codified

that people who marry deserve more and better than anyone else. Which, frankly, is bullshit.

It was a conundrum, this concern, warring as it did with the side of me that has been planning my gay wedding since childhood. (I was the only fifth-grade boy I knew with a notebook devoted to drawings of weddings, including lots and lots of sketches of other boys at my school.) This was a battle I was fighting on my own; whenever I'd start musing about the political ramifications, Jason would slip into a brief rhetoric coma until I was done. He talked about our getting married as if it was the most obvious thing, for in his logic, we *had* to do it for history. It would strike a political blow for equality, a slap in the face of craven politicians like George Bush and John Kerry who seemingly advanced their careers by pretending to believe that people like Jason and me aren't fully human. With Jason determined to marry, I sought balance between my opposing impulses: a conviction that there were other ways for the state to truly make people equal, and my burning desire to wed the man I'd been saying I was married to for nine years. The latter impulse being far more romantic, it is no surprise that I gave in to the notion very quickly—a little guiltily, maybe, but with excitement as well.

But then the actual deadline approached. Single straight people have often felt pressure from friends and family to marry, but I'm guessing very few can relate to a publicly announced date on which their entire state expects them to leap at the chance. This hit many gay couples like a tidal wave. After they had worked out the details of their unions on their own terms, damn it if the courts hadn't gone and upped the ante on them. For every couple who knew without question that nothing short of marriage would suffice, there were terrified lovers trying to do some fancy footwork to keep their partners from picking out the china just yet.

This dynamic was at work when we went to our favorite brasserie in New York with some friends, whom I'll call Jack and Ethan. They'd been a couple nearly as long as we had, and also owned a home together. Jack, who once came to a *Scarlet Letter*–themed party wearing the letter "I" pinned to his sweater to define himself as impish, had a glass of wine in hand and a gleam in his eye when he asked The Question. "What are you boys going to do about the whole marriage thing?"

Neither Jason nor I answered for a moment. I realized that Jason had stopped talking about the marry-for-history concept in the previous weeks and that I, who'd been won over to the idea, had known in my heart that he was having some reservations. At the table, we did what clever conversationalists do: we muttered something noncommittal and turned the tables, asking about Jack and Ethan's nuptial future. Ethan didn't say a word but stared down into his plate of steak frites, his cheeks reddening as he searched the meaty hieroglyphs for hidden meaning. Jack made a few jokes and dismissive comments as if to say it really just wasn't their deal, while Ethan kept quiet. It was a relief when the talk turned to a musical we'd seen, a safe—if incredibly gay—subject of conversation.

Newly equipped as Jason and I were to talk things out, our drive home from New York involved difficult emotional terrain. I asked Jason how he was feeling about getting married and he admitted he was having second thoughts, though he couldn't explain why, even to himself. All my politics aside, I had to fight the instinct that this was a rejection of some kind. I've lived in our culture far too long to be completely immune to the idea that being legally committed means being *truly* committed, as insane and false as I know that premise to be. And then there was the matter of pride: I'd laid aside my initial political concerns and, in the three months since, had told everyone we *would* be getting married. Now we wouldn't?

May 14 was the big day, and the Boston news coverage was full of crowds cheering for bride-on-bride smooches. After the day had come and gone, Jason and I were no closer to a decision, but that didn't rock our foundation as it once might have. What happened instead is that we were getting closer to an important understanding, which took shape in nightly conversations at the picnic table in our backyard. As the first warm evenings of summer came, we often ate dinner out back together, a quietly romantic enterprise, despite the half-inch coating of Deet that I wore to avoid being consumed whole by mosquitoes. As these evenings passed, our conversations grew richer and deeper.

What exactly was legal marriage? It was no guarantee of a lasting union, that's for sure. Both sets of our parents had divorced; my brother had divorced twice and Jason's was headed for his first. And, as we'd already proved, we were perfectly capable of splitting up without a license, thank you. So what was it?

As far as we could tell, legal marriage was a set of prizes and protections. The prizes were fiscal, largely resulting from employment benefits that could be shared with another person without question; the protections, from hospital visitation rights to right of survivorship in matters of property, were logical ways to recognize an established relationship. But no one on either side of the political debate had ever addressed why these perks—generated as they are from one's own work, earnings, and taxes—couldn't simply be directed wherever the worker who paid for them desired. If you're a single woman who has contributed years to your company and income to your state, why do you need a dress and veil to decide how those contributions should be applied? Why do so many believe that only people who marry—say, Britney Spears, seasoned pro that she is—are grown-up enough to have their relationships recognized? These questions had been passed over in favor of an easier-to-grasp concept: if straight married people get benefits, gay people should have the chance to get the benefits too. I could see the equality of that claim in specific, but the logic behind the overall system escaped me.

Now it was up to us to decide whether or not to enter that system. Because we lived in Massachusetts, Jason and I had been fortunate enough to replicate most of these elements already: making each other legal proxy for business and medical purposes, working for companies with domestic partner benefits, and living in gay-positive communities. We lacked federal tax protections, but I didn't mind that so much, as I was against the government's offering wedding-ring–based incentives anyway. The only arena in which we could see marriage offering a sanction we couldn't provide for ourselves was in the realm of parenting: if a child doesn't come out of your womb, the more paperwork you have that establishes your connection, the better. No one questions a valid marriage license when you show up at your child's school, or a hospital, or anywhere else. But, as we had no kids, this was a moot point.

If we weren't marrying for the benefits, that left only the emotional piece. But we both had come to understand that legal marriage was *not* the defining characteristic of real commitment. As the summer blossomed around us, we were growing ever more resolute that our future was going to be shared. We knew we were sure to have more conflict in years ahead, and find ourselves caught off guard by things we could not yet imagine. But we also knew that we intended to face that future together, no matter how hard the work. Jason said he couldn't explain why he felt like marriage might change that, but, at the same time, he did know that he wanted to be with me. And years of wedding planning or not, I knew what I really wanted: to grow old with Jason. This, then, was the biggest question that couples like us were facing: if you aren't getting married, will you still stay together? For us, the answer was clear: absolutely.

Don't get me wrong. It was progress for gays and lesbians to be able to share in a part of our culture that had long been denied us. And we knew that many couples who had fewer protections in place around their relationships than we did would benefit mightily from the chance to marry. That we chose to reject the option for the moment was just the fruit of new liberty in action: freedom doesn't mean taking advantage of every possible right and privilege—it means having the choice to do so if you wish. It was heartening enough to know that, should we ever want to walk down the aisle, our entire state was ready to throw the rice in celebration.

Lowering the importance of marriage relative to the place of commitment in our lives, we felt more secure than we had in several years, despite it being a tight time economically. I didn't have a class during that summer session, and Jason, having taken a year off from teaching to be an underpaid no-benefits pastry chef, was scraping by on a trickle of income from a few private speech-therapy clients. We were, as seemed to happen every August, coasting on fumes financially, but we were clearly back in the trenches together, and it felt good. When my mom's car died and she instinctively turned to us for help, it was a terrifying prospect, but we solved the problem as a couple. I scoured the want ads and Craig's List for a used car that could be paid for in accumulated laundry quarters, and Jason checked it out before driving it back to our house.

Broke or not, we even threw an end-of-summer party that brought together all the friends who'd seen us through the difficult period, from Courtney, the coworker whose shoulder Jason cried on during our separation, to Harry, whose friendship had remained strong. But this time there was no painting in the attic. Our friends saw the truth: a schmaltzball and a pragmatist who had fallen apart, picked up the pieces, and lived to tell the tale. That night we mixed up mojitos, passed plates of roast pork, and explained a dozen times that, no, we weren't getting married, and, yes, we were happy nonetheless.

And then a funny thing happened. I started thinking about children. I couldn't explain it, having buried that impulse for many years as other things became more important. My playwriting career was just taking off, which required a lot of time and effort, both for submissions and to attend stagings. I had also developed a desire to travel, which had led Jason and me to book a decade-late honeymoon in Paris for our upcoming tenth wedding anniversary. It's not as if my life felt empty and I needed a child to fill it. Hell, we barely even had down time. And yet, I kept thinking that Jason and I were ready to be a good family for a kid somewhere. When I raised the subject,

Jason surprised me by saying he'd been thinking the same thing lately. And just like that, years after our last discussion of the topic, a child returned to our mental picture of the VGs.

Perhaps, subconsciously, we were preparing to add to our family because our extended family was getting smaller. Nana, Jason's beloved grandmother who had sewed our wedding vests, was dying. She had been wrestling with terrible pain for some time. Finally, controlling her exit as skillfully as she ran all things in her life, Nana put her foot down with the doctor: she didn't want any more life-prolonging treatments. She wanted the morphine kept at the ready and, when the next struggle came, she wanted to slip away, having made the most of her eighty-six years.

A few days before she died, she began calling the family together at her nursing home because she knew her trip was soon to end. Jason and I, the last to arrive at her sunny room, were shocked at how frail she seemed, but were also inspired to see her still feisty and even elegant to the last. As she changed her earrings to a pair better suited for daytime and then moved along a chatty hospice worker who was taking up too much of her now extremely precious time, she was still completely Nana.

I couldn't help but think of my own Grammy's passing soon after Jason and I had married. On her last Friday alive, she had worked in her garden, sorted clothes for the church charity, folded bulletins for the weekend church services, and then, when all her tasks were done, had a heart attack. When my brother and I arrived in her hospital room in Maine that weekend, she apologized for the fuss and told us to head back home to Massachusetts, as she wasn't going anywhere. Then, not especially gently, she criticized the nurse for being so slow bringing her meal. My brother and I laughed about what the poor nurse was in store for as we headed for my brother's car and began the drive south to Massachusetts. Grammy died before we were home.

Ten years later, Nana held on a few more days after Jason and I made our final visit. Her granddaughter Chris bravely shepherded her through the final hours of morphine and pain and more morphine. Because we were not there when Nana died, what Jason and I were left with was a memory of Nana being herself to the end—a wonderful thing. Driving home from her funeral, Jason raised the prospect of giving our future child Nana's name.

Just before Thanksgiving 2004, Jason and I attended an adoption information session at a local library, intended to help couples choose between domestic adoption, foreign adoption, and DSS (Department of Social Services). We sat in a semicircle with two straight couples, one a military pair who'd been trying to get pregnant for years, and the other an older couple who already had one child and wanted another but didn't want to try a later-life pregnancy. We'd gone to the session thinking DSS would be the route for us, as domestic adoptions can take years, and no foreign countries at that time were knowingly allowing gay couples to adopt together.

There was another reason I wanted to go through DSS, though: I was scared to death of getting a baby—a tiny thing without language, who would be utterly dependent on me and unable to say what it needed. Instead, I had a vision of a two- or three-year-old, a little being who could say, "I'm crying because I pooped my pants and you haven't changed me quickly enough."

But the cheerful adoption specialist kept mentioning details about DSS that terrified me: we had to consider personality types like "antisocial" or "fire-starter." Then, she added how much easier it would be if we adopted two or four or six siblings at once. Worse, children under five were almost never available, and when they were, because of the state's extremely long reunification period, most were only available for fostering and wouldn't be up for actual adoption for years, if ever. It was one thing for us to think of helping provide a good home for a child who had difficult issues to face, but I knew in my heart I wasn't up for getting a half dozen of them merely on loan.

It was actually the speaker's attempt to be gay-positive that pushed me over the edge. When asked how our sexual orientation would affect our chances, she explained that we'd be perfect for a DSS child who had been so traumatized by his mother that it wasn't appropriate to have a woman in the home at all. Considering how greatly our female friends outnumber our male friends, that seemed a risky logic for placing a child with us. And it hit me. If we adopted an older child, someone else would have already set the child's mental image of what home, family, and parents meant. Yes, adoptive parents face that all the time, but is that what I wanted? I found myself thinking about a baby for the first time, and how I could be there from the beginning—scared shitless, mind you—as he or she discovered a loving, safe world to grow in. If I had the chance to do that, why wouldn't I?

Jason, as ever, was way ahead of me. He'd been wanting a baby all along and figured I would catch up. We decided that, no matter how long the wait, we'd go the domestic adoption route and raise a baby as a VG from the start. That long-forgotten third folder was to finally get some use, and we made a plan to begin the process after our trip to Paris.

Then, to my surprise, Jason proposed. And because he is the man he is, he did this between lights while driving.

It was the night after the adoption information session, and we were just approaching an intersection when Jason took a deep breath. It was dark in the car, and he kept his eyes on the stoplight as the car slowed and he began. "If we're going to adopt, maybe we should get married after all."

This was not a casual comment and I knew it; I could tell from the way he kept both hands on the wheel and tried not to look over at me. My heart leapt—I admit it, I was thrilled that he was asking. Intellect be damned, the fifth-grade girly boy in me was jumping up and down, waving a notebook full of grooms. But that was on the inside. The light had changed, and, since I didn't want the man I loved to drive off the road because of my reaction, I kept my voice quietly, happily calm.

"I think you're right," I replied.

A silence followed in which I could sense Jason's heart rate tripling. He managed to say, "And we could do it before our trip to Paris." He paused, the first real question of his tiny speech, "If you'd like that."

"I would," I said, trying not to cry and thus deter him from ever again taking initiative. "I'd like that very much."

And on we drove, the past dark behind us and the future bright ahead.

Where Babies Come From

12

∽

The Greatest
Sales Pitch Ever

IN THE PAST, AS A TEACHER FOR BOTH PRIVATE ACADEMIES and at-risk youth programs, I was always amazed and horrified at how easy it was for teenagers to conceive a child, typically without meaning to. The times I found myself helping anxious teens buy home pregnancy test kits, I'd hear tales like this one: the smitten young lovers hurried through their first fumble in the back row of a school bus, a brief event which they celebrated by going to McDonald's for Happy Meals (because the guy was collecting the action figures), both of them blissfully unaware that their six minutes of almost pleasure would yield a new life. It is a cruel joke that people not even thinking about pregnancy always seem to get pregnant with the least effort.

The majority of our adult friends who wanted children did not have such an easy time. The universe, sticking to its rule of not promising anyone anything, sometimes refuses to grant children even to wonderful people who would make good parents. Miscarriages, infertility, and other physical problems have conspired to send friend after friend to in vitro clinics or in search of sperm donors. Most times this led to the eventual birth of a child, but not always. Even when those techniques failed, none of our friends had ever pursued adoption.

For Jason and me, entirely womb-deficient from the word go, we'd never considered any other route seriously at all. Sure, there were a couple of other options, but I was against both. First, a friend of Jason's discussed the possibility of raising a child with us; but as much as I loved her, I knew I was way too much of a control freak for three-way parenting. We actually know a tri-parent family, who truly do the best job with their kids of anyone I've ever known, but that's about them and not me. It had taken a decade, a break-up, and countless hours of therapy to get me ready to handle a child with Jason alone, much less with an additional person I didn't even live with. We passed on option number one.

Option number two was surrogacy, which I know many people have pursued successfully for a host of reasons. Jason might have mulled this option longer, but I put the kibosh on it. No matter how nicely surrogacy was described, I always thought it came down to the idea that we would be intentionally creating a scenario in which our child didn't have his or her mother. It was one thing to react to a situation in which a mother could not keep her child and so expressed her love by placing her baby with us; it seemed another just to pay someone to produce and deliver goods like very high-end Chinese takeout. I would probably feel differently if I were part of an opposite-sex couple, a man and woman who knew this method would allow them to receive a delivery of their own egg drop soup. But it didn't apply to Jason and me, who figured that there were people producing babies just fine without our meddling. We'd be happy to step in at the other end of the process.

With adoption on at least our own mental horizons, we told our relatives both pieces of news: that we planned to legally wed on our tenth wedding anniversary and then to start the adoption process as soon as we were back from Paris. Their reactions were completely predictable. My brother—a church-going, Bambi-hunting marine and father of three—laughed out loud, envisioning how much children would change the lives of the Paris-going, brie-hunting homosexuals who were fathers only to a six-pound poodle, Sasha, whom we had adopted the Christmas before. Jason's mother, Nancy, who has always supported us, warmed to the idea slowly for some reason, while his aunt, uncle, and cousins were enthusiastic from the first word. His stepmother, Linda, was ecstatic, and his dad, being his dad, let her be. My mother, of course, didn't say a word. She didn't ask a question and offered little beyond, "Oh." She didn't say she thought we'd be bad parents, or that God was going to smite us. She just waited me out until I changed the subject or got off the phone.

Then, we told our friends, news which generated happy reactions in all corners but one: when we called our friend Ben, he actually groaned aloud. Ben and Abby, who married a few years after we did, were our closest couple friends, and we had spent many hours cooking for each other and swapping stories. But Jason and I didn't know at the time the painful thing that they were wrestling with when we weren't at their table: they had suffered multiple miscarriages. When we told them we were going to adopt, it hit like a bomb. Fairly or not, they had thought of us as the safe couple, their haven away from newborns and toddlers and baby talk in general. And here we were, entering the fray. The only consolation was that our process was expected to take forever; we all hoped that their conception and our match (adoption lingo for getting picked) would both occur soon enough that we could all celebrate without the pain of one couple being left behind.

Before we got anywhere with adopting, Jason and I had one little detail to take care of: legally marrying. It felt a little strange to walk into the Malden city clerk's office that December day and fill out the request for a license, and then to go to our doctors' offices for our blood tests after that. These rituals had been forever associated in my mind with straight couples. The blood test, it seemed to me, ought to remain so: it seemed comically useless for a couple biologically unequipped for procreation. But once we were officially marriage-ready, we called a justice of the peace and set the date for—when else?—New Year's Eve.

Because we had already had a real wedding ten years before, we didn't want to make a fuss with another one. We decided to marry in the living room of close friends in Somerville, the city we had lived in after our first wedding. Wearing suits and ties (this time I remembered my pants, thank you very much), we looked every bit a decade older, and the brief ceremony we had written for ourselves suggested that we might be a little wiser this time, too.

Before our witnesses, the justice of the peace read our words: "It is not a new life that begins today, but a chosen and hard-won life that continues to evolve with this step of legal marriage. David and Jason had a wedding ten years ago, in love with each other and the young idea of love. Today, they have a richer understanding of the challenges and rewards of love, and enter into this marriage as different men than those who entered the first. They choose this legal union with an eye especially toward the future and their hope to raise a child together, to bring a new person into the very small family of the Valdes Greenwoods."

Then he asked us to make our new vows. "Will you both undertake to sustain one another, to fight for your love when the going is rough, to cherish your own individual identities, to speak what must be said, and to honor all that you love in each other?"

Holding hands, we replied, "We will."

We didn't exchange rings at this point, because we were still wearing the ones we had purchased so long ago. Like us, they looked older than they once did, but their simple beauty was richer for still being on our fingers. We had fought hard to keep wearing these rings and we would continue to.

The justice of the peace closed our legal marriage ceremony by reading the last lines of *Angels in America* by Tony Kushner, in which the protagonist blesses the audience with the best thing he can think of: more life. Remarking that he felt like he could learn a thing or two about marriage just from our vows, the justice of the peace finally pronounced us husband and husband. Then, because I am me, I turned to Jason to surprise him by singing the very song Tuck & Patti were performing the first time we had ever held hands, which was also the song I had later proposed to. And because Jason is Jason, he really wasn't surprised at all. But he looked at me with such love and such pride in our making it so far, that my heart was full. His eyes were wet and I, of course, had tears streaming down my face, as we kissed and held each other. We raised glasses of champagne to history, both making it and living it, and turned our attention to the business of a proper honeymoon.

Paris was everything we imagined, from the afternoon light making the bridges on the Seine glow, to the cosmopolitan bustle of stylishly dressed people from all over the world clustering around café tables over coffee and cigarettes. We ate rich foods, made love, wandered about discovering centuries-old neighborhoods not in the guidebooks, and generally soaked up the city like an intoxicant, knowing this trip for what it would be: the last hurrah before parenting. It would not be so easy to just fly off and see the world again for a very long time, so even as we reveled in our journey, we were already looking ahead to the adoption beyond it.

Mind you, adoption would never happen if we didn't pick an agency. Task-hog that I am, as soon as we returned from Paris, I printed out a list of all the adoption agencies in Massachusetts, then removed any agency whose title referenced Jesus, the Virgin Mary, or Saint Anyone. I'm sure those businesses have all matched many happy families, but I just didn't feel like calling them up to find out how their particular God felt about my particular husband. Unfortunately, these agencies accounted for the majority of the ones in the state. Then, I deleted from the list any that were not licensed agencies but merely brokers or lawyers offering adoption services; the last thing I needed was to pay someone else to find me a baby they themselves could not complete the adoption of. Lastly, if an agency, even licensed, was actually just one very busy person with a secretary, I scratched the name off the list.

My winnowing reduced the number of options to two. That both startled me and made choosing much easier. One of the two charged 10 percent of Jason's and my combined income plus hourly fees for home study, placement, and finalization. My eyes glazed over as I tried to imagine what that would rise to. The other agency took the Club Med approach: the fee was all-inclusive. Whatever the costs along the way, one check took care of it all. I liked the idea of not doing any math during the process, so I called the agency, Adoption Resources of Jewish Family and Children's Service of Greater Boston, to find out just how big that check might be.

I immediately liked the woman who answered when I called. Betsy was clearly a cheerleader for adoption, staying cheerful even as she warned that it often took twelve to fourteen months to get matched. When I made some unhappy gurgling noise in reaction to that prognosis, she pointed out that sometimes it might go faster if we were open to a child of color. "Of course we are," I blurted, thinking to myself, "Well, *duh.*" But the woman admonished me for my surprise.

"You have no idea how many people will not consider a child of any other race but their own," she said. "They'll wait as long as it takes." This struck me as unbelievable. Considering the stories of the couples we knew, I couldn't imagine waiting through years of painful reversals and setbacks only to reject a child because of pigment.

This was, I suppose, a little hypocritical because of my background. To most Americans I have always passed as visibly Anglo, but I am half Cuban and half mongrel American. And my fondest wish was to adopt a child who, like me, was of mixed ethnicity. In fact, whenever I pictured a baby, I saw a little Latina with curly hair and big brown eyes.

Meanwhile, Jason's vision of a baby was premised on a little boy he had worked with years before, an African-American cutie who charmed the pants off everyone he met. So while I was mentally rocking our tiny Latina girl to sleep, he imagined bouncing our black son on his knee. I suppose then, in that way, we were a little like those prospective parents who have imagined themselves receiving a white baby, but there was a big difference: we weren't going to attach a paint chip to our application and force the agency to wait until they could match the exact color.

This willingness to adopt the first healthy baby that came our way clearly delighted Betsy. And I took hope from her enthusiasm: if most couples were spending many months angling to adopt from the same pool of babies, maybe we'd be able to adopt faster by not giving a damn about the color of the skin beneath the onesie.

The discussion of being open to children of any race somehow managed to obscure the initial reason for my call: finding out the cost. I hung up thinking adoption would cost us sixteen thousand dollars, a figure which had been mentioned in conjunction with a special agency grant program which might or might not even apply to us. Sixteen thousand sounded like a lot of money, and we realized we would have to sell our condo. But we figured that, even after we paid the adoption fee, the remaining profit from the condo sale would leave us with enough to put a down payment on a new place in a slightly more kid-friendly town than Malden, where the ratio of pubs to parks was skewed decidedly boozeward. Even before we signed the contract with the agency, we put our townhouse up for sale; it was a hot market at the time and we were optimistic.

It was March before we completed our paperwork to start the adoption process. We were sitting in the office of the agency director, Janet, when she referred to some future cost as "part of the twenty-seven thousand." Twenty-seven thousand what? When I realized she meant dollars, I blanched. I know I'm not good with numbers, but I hadn't ever gotten things wrong by eleven thousand dollars before. Our house was already on the market and I'd made an error equivalent to one fifth of my annual income. Even if we sold the condo for a profit of eighty thousand, as we expected, there was no chance in the Boston market that we'd have enough for both an adoption and a 20 percent down payment for a house. A lot of things went through my head at once, though they can be summed up neatly in a single syllable: *crap.*

We did not like the idea of renting again, taking a step backward in our financial security just as we were becoming parents. But we had no interest in giving up the plan to adopt, and we really liked this agency. So I nervously asked whether we would be less desirable to birth parents, who select adoptive parents from the agency's profiles, or to Adoption Resources itself, if we went back to being renters instead of owners. Janet just laughed. "I think you guys look pretty good," she assured us. But she also reminded us that no matter how attractive our application was, there was no way to predict what would make someone pick us. And, as she pointed out, "No one will pick you until you have your letter written."

She was referring to what is known as a "Dear Birth Parent" letter, which we had to write to convince someone to trust us with her child. As you might imagine, this was tricky business.

Yes, I'm a writer, but like nearly everyone else of my generation, I've given myself over to the sloth-ennobling immediate gratification of e-mail, which is to an actual letter as "lite" is to "satisfying." Despite being a playwright and journalist, I was no letter writer—and hadn't written a personal letter in many years. Jason barely even wrote e-mail, let alone regular letters, so our epistolary skills had grown quite lax, even as we faced the challenge of writing a letter that would determine the fate of one life and dramatically alter the course of several others.

A little precision was obviously needed, but that was made difficult because our intended audience was maddeningly unclear. Defying the common stereotype of unwed teenage moms looking to place their babies, Janet pointed out that it could just as easily be a couple looking to find a home for their child. Age was irrelevant, as was marital status. That meant we had to write a letter that compellingly addressed either one or two single or married people of any age. Easy as pie.

Because we didn't know her or them, we had no sense of what she or they would like to hear. Theoretically, that's a good thing, as we wouldn't want to squeeze our personality to fit ideals that are not our own. At the same time, we were asking someone to consider taking a hugely emotional leap of faith with us, so you can imagine our intense desire to say exactly the right thing.

Since a glance at the photo accompanying the letter would make it clear that there were two Y chromosomes in this couple, we knew some birth parents would instantly remove us from consideration. But we obsessed over what other details might send the wrong message. We wondered whether saying we loved our poodle would make us sound like those people for whom pets are indistinguishable from children—*not* the message we wanted to send to a birth parent. If we said we threw great cocktail parties, would the reader envision a debauched future culminating in Al-Anon membership for our child? If we said we both had advanced degrees, would we need to balance that with a mention of our addiction to *America's Next Top Model*, and hope the result painted us as neither too elite nor too moronic?

I found myself beginning to use Disney logic. By that, I mean an aesthetic that aims to avoid offense at all costs. From its movies to its Broadway shows, every Disney joke, plot line, and character is vetted so thoroughly for the potential to piss people off that the outcome is the artistic equivalent of plain custard: it hasn't got much flavor, but it's sure easy to swallow.

At the same time, we knew in our hearts that we couldn't write the plain custard of "Dear Birth Parent" letters. We wanted to somehow come across on the page in the way we saw ourselves in real life: goofy, punchy, and extremely loving. Honestly, what I really wanted to say in all capital letters was this: WE WOULDN'T SUCK.

Instead, we began a little more gently:

Dear Birth Parents,
Our names are David and Jason and we've been thinking about you a lot. That's funny, since we've never met you, and don't even know your names. But we do know that you're considering a brave and thoughtful choice, and we're

inspired by that. For some time, we've been thinking what we would say to you to help you know us better. So, as the song says, "Let's start at the very beginning . . . "

After a solid week of writing and rewriting, we finished the letter, along with a colorful booklet filled with photos of our lives, which prospective parents would only see if we had managed to hold their interest with our letter. Once both of these pieces had been turned in to the agency, we tried to distract ourselves from thinking about adopting by gearing up to move.

In April, having sold our condo, we rented an apartment in Arlington, Massachusetts, the kind of stroller-happy town which seems designed entirely for the breeding and rearing of children. If you have no child but want one, living in a place like Arlington can feel either encouraging or madness-inducing, an enormous civic taunt of "Nyah, nyah, you don't have a baby." The latter effect was heightened by our huge new apartment, which had a nursery and a sunroom for a child to play in—but no baby to fill either.

I felt that absence keenly. Having legally married, honeymooned in Paris, started the adoption process, sold our home, and moved in just over four months, I'd been so supremely busy that it was a blow to the system to suddenly have no task at hand. Not knowing when or if we'd get a match, we had nothing left to do but wander around our too-big apartment or walk the toddler-crowded streets, trying not to think about the year ahead, which stretched emptily before us in my imagination. If a man can feel his biological clock ticking, I was. Having been perfectly content without a baby all these years, I suddenly feared that our lives would feel incomplete without one.

As the trees came into bloom that spring, I kept imagining that, despite the fact that we'd just entered the adoption pool, maybe our birth parent letter was being opened already. As I sat writing in the nearest coffee shop—I had four to choose from now—it wasn't easy to focus, wondering as I did where our letter had ended up. Jason, it turns out, was often zipping along country roads on his bicycle wondering the same thing. We could do nothing more but hope that wherever our reader (or readers) was (or were), she (or they) would finish the letter and know instantly that we'd be great parents, or at the very least, that we wouldn't suck.

13

This Is Wanting Something

WE HAD BEEN LIVING IN OUR NEW APARTMENT ALL OF TWO weeks, me bitching and moaning the whole time about how empty it felt, when the call came. I was in a Laundromat up the street trying to find one damn dryer that actually lived up to its name, when my cell phone rang and Janet asked me if I was sitting down. I wasn't but I suspect the question was rhetorical anyway. Eight weeks into what was supposed to be a year-long process, we'd been matched.

A thirty-something mother of three working on a rural horse farm, Bella hardly fit the birth mom profile that we'd imagined. And we'd never have predicted the factor which had most strongly influenced her choice. Having read our letter and booklet, she'd picked us on the strength of how often we cooked big meals. Family dinners had been one of Bella's favorite things growing up, and when she saw evidence of such happy times around our table, something clicked.

She was due just two weeks later and hoped we could be there for the birth. With time so short, we started calling our relatives and friends to tell them the good news, despite Janet's warning that Bella could change her mind—not just right up until the birth, but after. Until she actually signed what is known as the surrender, the baby was no closer to living with us than any other child we'd never met.

In the meantime, we got snippets of Bella's story. She had called our agency in Massachusetts—hundreds of miles from where she lived—because no one in her hometown even knew she was pregnant. Digging up her baggiest old sweatshirts, she'd managed to let blousy material hide her weight gain as the due date approached. Having twice considered abortion and changed her mind, she nonetheless didn't want to disrupt her other children's world by announcing a new sibling who didn't have the same father as they did. Her older children, whom she loved deeply, lived primarily with other family members. Bella had a hard time financially keeping herself afloat, much less supporting a family. At the time of the birth, the water had been turned off in her apartment—not the ideal home for a newborn—and she had no working car.

Despite Bella's desire to pull off a completely unnoticed pregnancy, Janet logically insisted that she get counseling and assistance from a local agency near her home as well. That scared her, perhaps making the whole thing seem more tangible, or making her fear she'd be found out after all. As soon as we got matched, she blew off first one and then a second scheduled meeting with her local social worker. Yet whenever Janet spoke to her, Bella claimed she still wanted things to go forward.

The following days were deeply unsettling. I found myself listening to the song "The Beauty Is" from the musical *The*

Light in the Piazza. Considering the plot of the show involves an unhappily married woman helping her brain-damaged daughter wed an unsuspecting foreigner with a limited grasp of English, it's hardly the place to turn for inspirational messages about parenting. But the original context of the song didn't matter to me, as I couldn't help but feel the longing so clearly expressed in its lyrics: about what it feels like to want something so badly that you reach for it; about taking risks in hope that the moment of beauty will arrive. The words egged me on to keep hoping, but the tune was full of heartbreak, which I was afraid we would face. I played it for Jason and, a good sport always, he tried to find it touching, but he was too anxious himself to have energy left over for my melodramatic side.

As Bella continued to avoid the local agency and even Janet's calls, we began to understand how seriously she doubted her choice. Though we tried grimly to prepare ourselves, we felt crushed when Janet called five days later to tell us it wasn't to be. Both agencies agreed that Bella wasn't likely to follow through with the adoption, and they thought we should move on. Janet promised to keep shopping our letter around, and told us not to take it too hard, reminding us that eight months would've have been a fast match, let alone eight weeks. That's a little like telling a lottery winner to hand back his oversized check because someone got a number wrong; if you're the one stuck handing back your millions, you can be forgiven for not taking much comfort in the knowledge that the odds against you winning in the first place were huge.

Nonetheless, Bella, whom we could not picture, filled our minds the following week and the week after that. As her due date came and went, we couldn't help but think what might have been. Shortly after that, we marked another sad milestone: it was Nana's birthday, the first one since her passing at the end of the previous summer. A kind of malaise settled over the apartment. Though I knew this first match had been unlikely in its speed, still I couldn't shake it off.

When I called my mother and told her the match had fallen through, my voice was thick and heavy, and she was immediately concerned, though confused as to what could be upsetting me so. "So what's really the matter?" she asked. *What's really the matter?* "It has to be more serious than the baby," she went on, suggesting maybe Jason and I were having problems. I couldn't get off the phone fast enough.

Maybe it would have been healthier to let go of this failed match more easily, but Jason and I both nursed daydreams of getting a call out of the blue to say, "Surprise, surprise! Bella really did give birth and she still wants you to be the dads after all."

Which is exactly what happened.

One morning the following week, Jason didn't want to go to work. Jason is one of those people who goes for years without ever using up all his sick days. But as the end of the school year approaches, he really should take a few simply to preserve his sanity. By June, there's always at least one coworker who inspires his homicidal impulses and he turns into something of a Snark Monster. This is good neither for Jason nor his coworkers, nor for me, as I get to hear the full rant over dinner each night until the last blessed bell rings for the year. But on the first Thursday of June that year, he decided to do something about the annual insanity. At 6:00 a.m., he rolled over and drowsily announced he was going to take a mental health day. It was completely unlike him, but I didn't argue; I was excited at the prospect of our spending the day together, anywhere but in the too-empty apartment.

He'd just hung up from calling in "sick" to his school's answering service, when the phone rang. His first thought was that somehow the school was checking up on him to see if he was really ill or just a big slacker.

It was Janet.

She wanted us to come to her office as soon as we could. Jason sat up in bed, and I knew who the caller must be simply from his excitement. I leaned in to hear what I could of the conversation. The baby—a girl!—had been born earlier that week, and Bella wanted to talk to us by phone before she checked out of the hospital.

Dressed hurriedly, hardly able to breathe, we drove through the pre–rush hour streets along the very same route on which Jason had proposed to me. Halfway to the agency, we realized what Janet had said: the baby had not been born the week before, as expected, but just this week. I dared to say aloud what we were both thinking. "What if Bella had delivered on Nana's birthday?" Could the universe possibly align itself in our favor that much? It could indeed. The baby had been conceived the week Nana died and born on her birthday. Except for the fact that I didn't believe in providence, this was providence.

In Janet's office, we talked by phone to Bella for a few minutes. She sounded tired, scared, and so vulnerable that we were instinctively worried for her. She had no friends there to support her, and her own mother had only found out about the baby because labor had started in the middle of the night, ruining Bella's not entirely logical plan to take a bus to the hospital when her water broke. *Someone* had to drive her, and in a town as small as hers it wasn't going to be an ambulance, which might have ended up noisily exposing her secret when she was almost home free. Being called for a lift to the hospital, then, is how Bella's mother learned the news. From what we were told, the ride was a little tense.

In the middle of our brief conversation with Bella, we heard a tiny cry in the background. Jason and I both lost the thread of the conversation for a moment because of that little voice. There are few words to describe how badly we wanted to see the baby; unfortunately, teleportation remains the stuff of science fiction—we couldn't just beam into that far-away hospital room. We had to make do with knowing she was out there: our girl.

Or so we hoped. Bella had seemingly disappeared once; nothing was to prevent her from changing her mind again. But, contradicting the anxiety in her own voice, Bella claimed to be determined. She was checking out of the hospital, letting the baby go home with the agency's foster care family until we could get there. If all went according to plan, she would sign the surrender the next day, and that would be that. Once Bella hung up, though, Janet encouraged us to book a flight for after the signing, not before.

Knowing time was of the essence, Janet gave us a very short list of items to buy: a car seat, a pack of onesies, a bag of diapers, and a bottle of formula—that is, as soon as stores were even open. We raced home, scooped up our dog Sasha, and headed off to one of those homogenous plazas designed specifically for our age demographic: a Home Depot next to a

Target next to a Babies "R" Us. We sat in the parking lot like antique nerds at an estate sale, salivating in anticipation of the doors opening, and finally hurried inside to shop. We had all morning, so we figured we'd not only fill Janet's list but register for all the things we'd need in the months ahead. Once inside, of course, we were told politely that we could not be rolling a toy poodle, however small and cute, through the store in a shopping cart, and that we would either have to leave her out-side or leave ourselves. Sasha wasn't a sit-outside-tied-to-a-pole kind of dog, and it was June—if we left her in the car, we'd have PETA people breaking the glass to free her before calling the cops. Jason took the poor thing back to the car and I gath-ered up our paltry list by myself.

Back at home, we tried to compose a registry online, which is a bad idea if you are a child-rearing novice and can't picture half the items in real life. We signed up for dozens of items we were sure we would need later, but some of what we registered for was useless clutter-making crap: for instance, the break-away feeding pad, an item which turned out to be ideal for people with, uh, breasts. We didn't yet know how many redun-dant, unwieldy, or parent-annoying products were out there, all of them praised by "real" people in suspiciously euphoric lan-guage on online bulletin boards.

Once shopping, registering, and packing were accomplished, we had nothing to do but fidget. Still, despite our sudden good news, we didn't call anyone. Having been left raw by the first "disruption," as adoption agencies gently describe it when a match falls through, we didn't want to wear our hearts on our sleeves again just yet. Instead, we busied ourselves with settling on the first gift we would give our daughter—her name.

As you might recall, we'd established on our second date that we would have a child someday, and we'd started imagining names for a hypothetical child fairly soon after. A boy would be Jonah something-or-other, and a girl would be Sophie Pilar. Jonah and Sophie had together been a part of our couple folklore for so long, it seemed unthinkable that we'd choose anything else. And yet, almost as soon as we'd filled out the adoption paperwork, we'd abandoned both names entirely.

For the two months since we'd signed our paperwork, we'd endlessly amused ourselves by playing the name game. An excellent distraction tool, we could play the game anywhere, though the locale of brainstorming affected the quality of the outcome. "How about 'Loofah?'" I might ask while showering.

But choosing a name wasn't really a laughing matter. We were newly haunted by our own past bad behaviors: the times we'd rolled our eyes at other people's baby names, snickering at what we saw as woefully misguided choices inspired by seasons, fruits, or even car parts. Now that the baby shoe was on the other foot, we began to consider that Summer, Apple, and Axle must have sounded perfectly logical to someone else. We knew, no matter what name we chose, some asshole like us would mock it too.

At the very least, we wanted to avoid becoming those parents immortalized in bad-name stories, the kind of funny-horrifying tale swapped at dinner parties. For instance, I once knew a girl named Inita (like Anita, but with an I) Mann. Her dad said he'd come up with the name because it was funny and he figured she'd only have to endure it for twenty years or so. (He was wrong, it turned out, on both counts.)

While Jason and I agreed we needed to replace Sophie and Jonah, we initially found our aesthetics weren't lining up very well otherwise. I'd champion some name from the island that my father's family left by boat forty years ago, while my sweetie countered with something a little more WASPy. For a brief moment, our two idioms did unite, in a boy's name at once a little ethnic and somewhat patrician: Xavier. I admit that it had a certain grandeur, at least until I began to overthink it. What would his nickname be? X? And wasn't it cruel of us to saddle a child with a four-syllable first name when our last name was already a two-word, four-syllable mouthful? The final straw was when I heard a teen mom on the subway address her little Xavier in pure Bostonese. "Egg-zay-vee-uh," she crooned, dropping the final r so the name now rhymed with "duh." On the principled grounds that I cannot give my child a name which sounds that bad in the dominant regional dialect, I took it out of the running, leaving the list of boy's names awfully slender.

Now, the birth of a girl had made that a moot point. We had, thankfully, gotten our list of girl's names up to five or six choices, including Simone and Serafina. When we first matched with Bella, we settled on a leading contender, but didn't dare tell anyone; before a baby is born, people feel perfectly free to gasp or roll their eyes at the names you pick, assuming either that you have no feelings at all or that you simply took a name you found in a fortune cookie and so could care less. In contrast, once the baby is real and before them, no one dares mock the name—at least in your presence. We vowed to keep our name choice secret, bandying about tasteful nicknames like Stinkalina Rose instead.

But now it was time to reveal the name. Bella told us that she had randomly picked a name herself in a panic during that first night at the hospital, but that she thought we should choose something which had more personal meaning. We didn't hesitate. Our daughter would take her middle name, like her birthday, from Jason's Nana—Ruth. For her first name, we settled on something simple enough to flow easily with our cumbersome last name and lovely enough that a little girl could say it without embarrassment and, we hoped, even with delight. Moreover, the name would gently bring to mind both Nana's favorite flower and the bright flower beds I loved that had surrounded Grammy's house when I was a boy.

Her name would be Lily.

Once you have given a baby a name and heard her tiny voice, there is pretty much no way to think that she might not actually be yours. The morning after the phone call, I was already writing a lullaby for her in the shower, practicing it over and over so I'd be ready to rock her to sleep. We packed our bags for the airport eagerly and left an empty bag just for Lily's things. But shortly before our cab was to come, the phone rang. Bella had skipped the signing altogether. No one knew where she was. Hating to say it, Janet told us to unpack.

There is something awful about an empty infant car seat. It's just about as tangible a metaphor as it can be, and it goaded us, sitting there in our empty sunroom. It wasn't truly equal to a death; we knew that absolutely. But it opened up a terrible hole in our hearts anyway. Worse, not having told anyone yet about our joy, we now had no one prepared to comfort us. When our friend Anjali came by the next day so that we could attend a neighborhood food fair, we first had to fill her in on the good news so she could then soothe us about the bad. I wasn't easily consoled, and as we walked up the street to the fair, I found the sunny day too much to stand. When we waded into the crowds at the food stalls, it got worse. Babies in Bjorns, toddlers with food on their faces, preschoolers tugging on the sleeves of their pregnant moms—we were as swarmed by little beings as if we'd landed in Oz. We didn't stay long.

If the house had seemed empty before, now it was a cavern, in which loss and confusion were mixed up with anger. How could this have happened? From the way Jason had spontaneously cancelled work minutes before the agency called us in, to the stunning birth date, the serendipitous coincidences had made this match seem destined; now, it seemed like the gods were mocking us.

The next day, Bella announced that she was going to keep the baby. Considering that we were heartbroken after hearing a single cry, how could we possibly not understand her wanting to be with the precious baby she had carried for nine months? Nonetheless, I couldn't help but worry that it wasn't a good idea. How could she care for the baby if she couldn't keep her water turned on? Living on her own out in the country with no car, what would she do in emergencies? Hour by hour, I'd remember the tiny voice of the baby I couldn't call Lily anymore and think, "We were supposed to be there now." But she wasn't our girl after all; as Jason reminded me, worrying about her was no longer our job.

Life went on. Jason's school year still had three weeks to go, and I had started teaching my one summer course. I had plenty of time on my hands for activities like walking the dog or cursing the size of our new apartment. A week after the re-disruption, I was filling a morning by cleaning the house in my underwear when I got a call from the Midwest agency. The social worker, Lisa, asked generally about my last conversation with Janet, and

I said that we hadn't talked since things fell apart. This seemed to throw Lisa, who said, "Well, I was just calling to see how you were," and hung up. Odd social skills, I thought, and turned the vacuum cleaner back on.

Barely a clean rug later, the phone rang again: the adoption was back on. Almost as soon as Bella had decided to keep Lily, she realized it was impossible. For one thing, she couldn't even get a ride to pick up the baby; Bella's mother didn't want to disrupt her routine and asked if they could reschedule a more convenient time, say, another day entirely. This was the final reminder to Bella of how ill-prepared she was to raise a baby at this moment in her life. After she realized this, both agencies had worked all week toward the goal of our adopting Lily at long last, but no one had told us, fearing we might face another disappointment. Inadvertently, they'd kept this secret too long: Bella was already at the agency signing the surrender and wondering when we'd arrive. When Lisa heard in my voice that we knew nothing about it, she'd panicked and hung up so she could call our agency to find out what the hell was going on. Janet, it turned out, had decided to wait till the papers were really and truly signed to tell us—a detail not shared with the other agency.

In the end, this caused sequential mini freak-outs: the social worker suddenly afraid that we weren't supposed to be the adoptive parents after all; Janet dismayed that someone else in her office, spurred by Lisa's call, got to reveal the news to us instead; and me, standing flabbergasted in my underwear, with a vacuum cleaner hose in one hand but no airplane ticket in the other, realizing I had to get to another state that same day. It was already one o'clock, so we had no time to waste. Jason left work—no need to make up an excuse this time—while I repacked us, booked a hotel, and got us seats on the last flight of the day that went anywhere near where we had to be.

At that moment, I had a realization: since the baby had already been discharged and was living with a foster family, this meant Jason and I wouldn't be able to take the new parent after-care class at Bella's hospital. We had read about the class online and, in the original plan, figured we be in town for those first few days after the birth, with time to take the class before Bella went home. When that first plan fell through, we figured we'd have many months at home to take some similar class elsewhere before we were matched again. Instead, now we would be flying to get a baby while knowing almost exactly nothing about what we were doing. We did have a copy of one of those "baby's first year" books, but I'd barely opened it. As Jason drove home, I furiously skimmed the book for tips on infant feeding, sleeping, bathing, and pooping, and then typed up a two-sided five-by-seven cheat sheet with bulleted instructions and emergency numbers. Yes, my inner control freak needed an owner's manual for the baby, and having one made me feel much better.

Two hours after Bella had signed the surrender, we got in a cab to the airport, making phone calls as fast as we could. We were actually sitting on the tarmac when I reached my mother, who knocked my socks off by saying that she'd been praying about the baby ever since the first disruption. Her only problem, she said, was that she hadn't known whether to pray that we would get the first baby or, if it was what God wanted, a different baby. The real message of her prayer, at least as I heard it, was that she was now on board with our adopting after all. Considering the nature of the day, I shouldn't have had any reserve shock left in me, but I did.

It was midnight, far too late to meet Lily, when we checked into a Residence Inn just off a midwestern highway strewn with every big-box retail giant and chain restaurant you've ever heard of. We unpacked our things, set up a hotel crib, and made a little baby nook in one corner, trying to cozy up the sterile room we'd be spending the next week or more in as we waited for the two states, ours and Bella's, to complete all the necessary paperwork for the placement. Drawing the blinds to dim the neon glow of TGI Friday's and Wal-Mart, Jason and I crawled into bed and spooned, knowing sleep was unlikely. It was our last night together as just a couple. In the morning, the Valdes Greenwoods would be a family of three.

14
∽

Two Madmen and a Baby

PEOPLE ENJOY SCARING PARENTS-TO-BE WITH TALES OF THE
life-altering madness which awaits them. These dire predic-
tions often have a solid basis in fact. The sleep-deprivation
thing, for example, is every bit as discombobulating as people
say (over and over and over). Similarly, the tales are true about
the eagerness of strangers, especially elderly ones, to touch
your child, with no regard for how many contagions their wiz-
ened fingers might introduce to the little blank slate of an immune system before them. On the other hand, everyone who
described the instantaneous love we'd feel for Lily was also
correct. I really did feel as if a whole new chamber had
opened in my heart, a secret room I couldn't have imagined
the size of, which was now the place Lily occupied.

But no one, and I mean no one, had mentioned at all the
most disturbing facet of the new experience: wanting, desperately, to give the baby back. Now, before nonparents drop this
book in horror—and, really, only a nonparent would be shocked

at that statement—let me assure you that we didn't actually return the baby to sender. But I'm getting ahead of myself.

The morning Lily came into our family, we were scheduled to arrive at the Midwest agency at ten o'clock. Being Valdes Greenwoods, we're early risers anyway; add impending parenthood to the mix and we were up before most of the chain restaurants were even flipping pancakes. To kill the time, we decided to eat at Bob Evans, a restaurant I hadn't even heard of, as soon as it opened. Jason assured me that a Bob Evans joint would provide a suitably definitive Midwestern dining experience, which we could think of as a tribute to Lily's roots. And, hell, wasn't it about time we started eating at family restaurants anyway?

Jason ordered biscuits and gravy, which he didn't finish, claiming that they were too salty, which he says every time he orders biscuits and gravy. I ordered . . . well, I have no idea. I didn't finish whatever it was, because I was too nervous, and I imagine that was the real culprit for Jason's lost appetite as well. In theory, new parents really should shovel in as much food as possible before they have a baby and thereafter find themselves eating whatever leftover take-out item is most easily removed from the fridge and consumed one-handed. But we didn't know that yet, so instead of eating, I scoped out the families around us. They were all, by Massachusetts standards, enormous: five or six kids of all ages squeezed into a booth with mom, dad, a grandparent or two, and maybe a grizzled uncle type in a John Deere cap who looked liked he'd rather be outside smoking. Our let's-go-Midwestern breakfast only heightened how unlike the local families we were.

Finally, the time came to meet our girl. We drove along a country road until we saw a small house with the agency's sign on the front lawn. Workers were setting up a benefit yard sale as we pulled up, and they nonchalantly nodded for us to head inside. As we walked through the door, I could see down a long hallway to a conference room, where a woman with her back to us was cradling a baby. Over the crook of the woman's arm, I saw a slip of pink dress: *Lily*.

The woman was Lisa, Bella's social worker, and I'll never forget the moment she turned around to introduce us to our daughter. With thick dark hair and big brown eyes, Lily looked just like the baby I had imagined for so long. Bella had led us to think that Lily's dad was white, but there she was, a beautiful biracial baby who could easily have been my offspring. Born weighing just over six and half pounds, and still coming in under eight, she felt absurdly light when Lisa settled her into the crook of my arm. Jason and I took turns holding her, saying her name over and over, both of us emotional. Lisa was unfazed, considering this is what she does for a living, and she busied herself with presenting gifts from Bella, Bella's mom, the foster mom, and even the old gals of the Ladies Auxiliary at the hospital. In eleven short days, already Lily had received so much love.

After Jason and I had passed Lily back and forth for fifteen minutes, awestruck with the newness of it all, Lisa gently said, "Okay then," clearly meaning, *You can go now*. We were both startled at the speed of what was happening; hell, no one had even asked for ID, though I suppose the odds were slim that any other gay couple would be appearing on this country lane before noon looking for a baby. Apparently noting our classic deer-in-headlights expressions, Lisa asked if we had any questions.

"Is there anything we should know about feeding or . . . " I trailed off hopelessly. Lisa assumed I was asking a specific question, not floundering in abject ignorance.

"Well, she didn't finish the last bottle, so she'll be hungry soon," she offered. As much as we wanted to freeze the moment in time, Lisa had other families to bring together. Unable to ease our entry into parenthood any further, she ushered us out of the office and into the sunlight.

Seeing Lisa's coworkers outside working the yard sale, Jason asked, a little embarrassed, "Does anyone know how the car seat is supposed to fit?" We tried to pass it off as a question that stemmed from the fact that we were driving a rental car, but honestly we just didn't know, period. The agency director came over to help us get set up, and then it was just us three. I climbed into the back seat next to Lily, who was so tiny that she didn't even reach the seat's inner headrest for newborns, and as we drove off into our new lives, I tried to keep her head from falling off.

The next few days were a loop of discovery in three-hour cycles: we discovered how much Lily could eat at once (two or three ounces), how long she'd be awake staring at the nearest lamp or grabbing our fingers (forty-five minutes to an hour), and how long she'd sleep (an hour or two), before starting the pattern over. We learned so much so quickly—that it is wise to have a fresh diaper underneath your baby before removing the previous diaper; that a baby's blackened belly button stump is deeply disconcerting to look at; and that letting a baby sleep skin-to-skin on your chest is just about the sweetest thing imaginable.

We'd been told it would take at least a week to get the paperwork approved for us to leave the state with Lily. First the local agency and our agency both had to sign off on the placement, then the paperwork had to be sent to state officials in Bella's state, which would send what is called an interstate compact to officials in our home state, who would then also have to consent. Not knowing for sure whether this would take seven days—or longer—made us restless. Fortunately, the infant car seat turned out to be an awesome invention, on par with fire and ready-made formula. Like a picnic basket stocked with the most adorable contents ever, the car seat could go anywhere we needed. At the nearest Babies "R" Us, we found a genius little invention called Snap-and-Go, a folding cart that became a stroller once a car seat was placed in it. Whenever the dark hotel room got to us, we just packed up our bucket o' baby and headed off to find ways to pass the hours. Fortunately, Lily had no idea where we were taking her: a cheesy mall, a vast Wal-Mart, a series of fast food restaurants. These excursions made the already surreal days feel even less like our daily home life, but we were glad simply to leave the four walls of our room. Even so, by the third day, we had exhausted all the local attractions except for hiking trails, which I had no intention of braving with a stroller.

It was also about that time that we began to wonder why Lily wasn't pooping. Our friend Ben finds it bizarre that everyone, from doctors on down, uses the term *poop*, but I find it completely logical. Considering how often new parents must discuss poop, do you really want to be accurate and say "excrement" all day long? Poop is harmless sounding, possessed of a certain charm that erases any memory of odors. If words can be adorable, *poop* is an adorable word. But however you spin it, Lily didn't poop. Not the day we got her, or the next, or the one after that.

The agency set up a doctor's appointment for us, and we had our first true taste of being parents. Yes, living with a baby round the clock for three days was parenting, but there is a difference when you enter a public sphere where someone else wants to poke and prod your baby. The doctor's affect was somewhere between church deacon and android. For a country doctor right out of Norman Rockwell, he did not offer any discernible human warmth. To measure Lily, he laid her out in just her diaper on his exam table, holding her head down with one hand and, no joke, grabbing her ankle with the other so that he could stretch her as far as she'd reach. She was screaming bloody murder, while he talked about something else entirely, seemingly unaware of either her shrieking or the way Jason and I had assumed lunge position, ready to throttle him. I might have beaned him with his own framed diploma, if I had thought it would be at all easy for two men and their baby to make a quick getaway.

Finally, he dispatched us with advice to try suppositories or prune juice or both. The rest of that day was spent trying to coax a poop out of our wee one. And when she finally yielded first a lump of coal and then a brackish mass, we cheered her on like proud parents at her first swim meet. You go, poopy girl! Let me just say, this was a new life.

Each night, we shared the day's news with Bella, who seemed eager to hear every detail. We finally set up a time to spend a few hours with her at a restaurant near, but not in, her hometown. The hour drive to her mother's farm was revealing; it turned out that where we were staying didn't yet remotely scratch the surface of country. Houses grew fewer and further between as we drove, while the number of barns and horses increased. I saw girls walking their horses in rolling pastures and wondered if Lily ever would. Yellow ribbons supporting troops fluttered from flagpoles. The trees were thick along the road, and the landscape a lush green. I tried to soak it all in so I could tell Lily someday.

As we neared our destination, we passed rustic churches whose signboards contained slogans like "He who kneels stands tallest" and "Know God, Know Peace; No God, No Peace." The houses, scattered as they were, boasted an equal number of now-outdated Bush and Kerry signs on their lawns. We only passed through one "downtown" area along the way, which consisted of a few red brick buildings and storefronts adorned with hand-lettered posters saluting the local high school team.

I was glad that Jason and I had both dressed for the occasion in what I thought of as—I hate to say it—nonthreatening attire: shirts from the Gap. Despite all my own past arguments about the dangers of social assimilation, I found myself wanting nothing more than to blend in. There have been countless occasions on which I've enjoyed making a flamboyant statement with an outfit—here a leather man-bag, there a polka dot ascot—but I had no intention of making any kind of splash while driving along unfamiliar back roads. Because we'd also be meeting Bella's parents, who were not crazy about the adoption in general, I had intentionally dressed in as neutral a fashion as possible; there'd be plenty of time for wearing sleeveless cowboy shirts when the baby was safely home in the land of gay marriage.

If we were dressed with an imagined Midwest aesthetic in mind, it seemed that Bella had tried to think what might strike a couple of gay guys as cool and fun. When she came into view, she was dressed entirely in baby pink: hip-hugging pink jeans the exact color of her T-shirt, which was emblazoned with a decal of a cowgirl. She had dyed blonde hair pulled back into a ponytail, which bounced as she ran down the steps to meet us. The effect made her seem younger than her thirty-some years.

Bella's parents looked like meeting us might kill them, Lily's grandmother squeezing out a tight smile, and her grandfather darkening visibly like a thundercloud. Me being me, I hugged them both and talked too much as they showed us around the two enclosures where their horses grazed. That helped to warm things up a bit, but it was a relief for all of us when they went their way and Jason and I were left with just Bella and Lily for lunch. We drove to a restaurant a half hour away so that Bella wouldn't run into anyone she knew, and we sat down to get to know each other over sandwiches that made the portions at Bob Evans look small.

Bella explained that her father had tried to talk her out of the adoption at the last minute. It wasn't our gayness, she said, but the whole adoption concept that was bothering him. He had become convinced that there was a verse of scripture against adoption that he just couldn't remember. But Bella disagreed. In fact, she believed that God had led her to carry the baby to term so a couple who had no other chance of becoming parents could raise the child. This touched Jason and me both, though this argument had left her father unpersuaded. She told us that he'd asked why, if adoption was such a good thing, it was never mentioned in the Bible. "Moses was adopted!" I crowed, to provide fodder for Bella's self-defense. Maybe I didn't know Midwest, but I have the Old Testament down.

Over the course of the meal, we swapped stories, as if we were on a three-person blind date. We learned that Bella's past had been a roller coaster of marriage and separation and re-union, punctuated by a period of cocaine use, followed by recovery and growth. We shared likes and dislikes, including her announcement that her favorite print was cheetah, a piece of information which struck me as singular, as it had never even occurred to me to *have* a favorite print. But the most profound thing about Bella was how much she loved her children; though she wasn't able to do most of the parenting herself, it was clear from her stories that her kids loved her too and were growing up well, despite her struggles.

This was further highlighted when we saw her with Lily. Already recognizing Lily's hungry cry, we asked Bella if she wanted to feed her. The way she settled the baby so naturally in one arm suggested years of mothering, and when she began absentmindedly rotating the bottle gently just enough to keep Lily drinking, I realized I was learning something about parenting from a woman who would never get to parent Lily herself. "My kids always say I need to have another baby," she said wistfully. "I wish I had told them sooner . . . but it's too late. They'd hate me if I told 'em now." She looked down at Lily and everything unsaid was loud and clear.

When we dropped Bella off, we stood a few feet away from the car while she leaned in to whisper her good-byes to the baby. Though we would remain in contact and even visit every year, we all knew what that moment meant. From the time we got in the car and pulled away, she really became the birth mom who had let her baby go, and we were now the parents. Yes, it's what Jason and I had hoped for, but we both cried for miles anyway.

With lack of sleep added to such profound emotions, Jason and I were feeling a bit manic. When we learned from the local agency that our seven days would become ten, we called for reinforcements. On the day we had originally expected to fly home, Jason's dad and stepmother, Jim and Linda, drove the four hours from their town to see us, with Jason's sister and cousin in tow. On the one hand, it was a joy to see people we knew and loved. On the other hand, it was a little insane. Linda's a planner, and she had us scheduled to go to a museum in the nearest big city one day, and then to a state park the next. I didn't honestly want to do either thing, but she was so eager and we were so exhausted, we rolled with it.

This particular museum, an hour away from where we were staying, was a special kind of hell for a new parent. Its primary exhibit hall was painted pitch black, with a combination of fixed lighting, neon, and strobe lights. Crowds swarmed up and down ramps and around a mazelike central chamber, a perfect recipe for madness if you are pushing a stroller. Lily alternately cried and slept, her tiny form jostled about as we tried to maneuver through people and displays. Instead of having nervous breakdowns, Jason and I begged off of seeing the rest of the museum and said we'd meet everyone outside later.

Because there hadn't yet been enough coincidence in our lives recently, when we walked out the front door of the museum, we stepped directly into the path of the city's gay pride parade. We were near a pier where the parade ended and the groups all had to pass us as they exited the route. No longer feeling nervous, as we had in Bella's rural hometown, we could finally relax about our appearance as a family. As you can imagine, two dads and their baby were made quite welcome here, especially by a church group bearing bundles of lilies. When they learned our girl's name, they festooned her stroller with deep red blossoms. Two weeks old and she was not only attending her first gay pride, she was a float.

The next day was our first Father's Day, which was exciting, except that the state park visit seemed a little doomed. It was a gorgeous day and every damn person in the state felt like taking a nature walk. A marathon search for two parking spots left us grumpy, and our cars had to split up to park. When we regrouped and tried to perk up, it turned out the only paved paths were made of crushed limestone, requiring us to move at a glacial pace so as to avoid reorganizing Lily's vertebrae. Our progress was so slow, we all gave up after less than an hour, and instead headed to the local diner for lunch. We had a much better time just sitting around, eating, and chatting, which is just what a family should do. And what a family: three Jews, two WASPs, and two people of mixed race; biological and adopted children; spouses straight and gay; three Democrats and a Republican.

To me, this seemed the perfect picture of the new American family, in which old divisions and norms are blurred, blended, and reinvented. But that concept may have exceeded the grasp of one fellow diner who came over and cooed at Lily. The woman was squeezing behind Jason's chair when she asked whose baby it was. I said Lily was ours, pointing at myself and then across the table just as the woman started to congratulate me. "Well, happy . . . " she got out before she realized that I was pointing not at Linda, but at Jason. The poor dear literally almost fell over. Grabbing the back of a chair and steadying herself, however, she did the right thing, quickly finishing her sentence, ". . . Father's Day," before fleeing.

To be honest, no one else batted an eyelash during our time in the Midwest. Old ladies and young girls surrounded Lily wherever we went, wishing us luck and offering advice. The hotel cleaning lady checked in on Lily every day and even brought her a teddy bear (which, oddly, said the Lord's Prayer in the creepy voice of the narrator on *Buffy the Vampire Slayer*). Even so, the warmth and friendliness couldn't obscure the fact that we weren't at home, and the wait grated on us as a week became ten days and then eleven and twelve. The state official who had gotten our paperwork had opened it, left it on his desk, and— so his coworker reported—gone on vacation. Similar delays held us up until we felt more than a little crazy.

On day thirteen, we were introduced to a quirk of interstate adoption law. The child welfare agency in Bella's home state had finally signed off on the paperwork for us to leave, but the officials couldn't fax the items to Massachusetts because the original signatures were required; instead, the documents were overnighted to the relevant office in Boston. Until Massachusetts officials actually received and signed the documents themselves, we could not enter the state. Here's the bizarre part: we could go to any other state in the union. As long as we weren't trying to sneak Lily into a state which had a formality to observe, she could go wherever we pleased. It made no sense that it was perfectly legal for us to take her to the Grand Canyon or the strip in Vegas, but not back to our apartment. We were advised to get as close to Massachusetts as we could without crossing any law-breaking border and just be ready to head home when the last form was signed.

Desperate for any motion, we did just that, catching a flight to Baltimore—no closer to Massachusetts than where we had started, actually—which could get us on a connecting flight to Providence, Rhode Island, less than an hour's drive from our place. We landed in Baltimore with ten minutes to run through the concourse—me swinging Lily in her bucket and Jason loaded down with baby gear—to our gate, which was ready to close. Hurrying down the airplane aisle to our seats, we could smell the inopportune truth: someone very small smelled like pee, and if we didn't change her now, she'd soon be the shrieking baby everyone fears being trapped on a plane with. As if we'd been doing this all our lives, we flipped Lily down onto the seat, whipped off one diaper and taped on the new, hoisted her into the air, and had ourselves belted in before the last overhead bin was clicked into place. I remember this move being accompanied by applause from our fellow passengers, but that may just be the hallucination of a tired man.

Fourteen days after our initial departure, someone we never saw signed our paperwork, and we left Rhode Island for home. A neighbor took a photo of us upon our return, standing in the driveway with Lily asleep in her car seat. The image is telling: Jason and I are both smiling, but Jason has bags under his eyes and my eyes are narrow slits, as if I am half sleeping upright. We didn't have a clue that, after all that, getting home was the easy part.

A week later, I was sure we had made the biggest mistake of our lives. The school year not quite finished, Jason had to go back to work for a few more days, and I was home alone with Lily, a big shift from those weeks in the hotel with my husband always just steps away. Even when he returned home from school, it seemed impossible to care for Lily and have the energy left to get meals made, care for our neurotic poodle, and keep on top of the mounds of cardboard and bubble wrap from the endless stream of baby products we'd received as gifts. We had no nearby relatives, so it was just us, and the sheer round-the-clockness of the situation was beginning to sink in.

I loved Lily. I knew this in my heart. But I couldn't get my head around the idea that I was going to be with her hour after hour, day after day, eternally trying to figure out what she wanted when she cried uncontrollably, while operating on roughly two good hours of sleep. I began thinking about my old life: going to movies on a whim, writing all day whenever I was inspired, even just taking a nap because I wanted to. That was all gone, I was sure of it, replaced by an endless replay loop of cries and consolation.

It didn't help that I hadn't understood beforehand that babies only a few weeks old can hardly see you, much less interact with you. Where were the coos and smiles? Where was the clear recognition that I was Papa, caring for her even when I was loopy with fatigue? In my least charitable moments, I thought: this isn't a baby; it's a blob I put things into and wipe things off of. I had expected my baby to clearly love me back and not just burp in my general direction.

One afternoon, Jason took Lily for a walk in the baby Bjorn and told me to try to squeeze in a badly needed nap. Instead of sleeping, I burst into tears. I didn't want to do this anymore. I envisioned scenarios in which Bella's home state decided we had to return the baby; we would of course comply, looking tearful, all the while secretly thrilling to the prospect of regular sleep again. But when Jason returned I kept mum, because I knew even having such thoughts made me the worst son of a bitch who ever lived.

Surprisingly, my meltdown had the unexpected effect of calming me down somewhat. Once you've thought the worst, there's nowhere to go but up. And not actually having abandoned my husband and child to join a circus or a cult, I realized that I might be able to cope after all. I was in a pretty Zen state a week later when I walked into the living room to find Jason in tears with the baby on his lap. He had become convinced that she wasn't responding appropriately—was she blind? Deaf? Or were we just bad parents? It poured out of him: he felt completely overwhelmed by our new lives and he didn't know if he could handle it.

I was so glad to hear this I could have danced for joy. Instead, I kissed him on the forehead and snuggled in next to both of them on the couch, where I revealed my own previous breakdown. "Why didn't you tell me?" he asked. I told him the truth: I was sure I must be a deeply deficient human being to entertain such thoughts, even for a second. It gave me comfort to know that, between us, there were at least two people this terrible in the world.

Later, we would hear "Can I give the baby back?" stories from pretty much every parent we knew. And biological children prompted this reaction in parents with exactly as much frequency as adopted kids. The truth of the matter is that children, especially first children, occasion a perfect storm of sanity-threatening conditions: daily lack of sleep, sudden recognition of a permanent change of lifestyle, and a host of intense emotions. This leads otherwise perfectly respectable folk to imagine doing wild things. One great mother we knew told us she'd had fantasies of leaving her baby in a stroller on a public bike path and running the other way. The good news is that so very few parents actually mean it, especially once they've had a few hours sleep. Most of us don't really want to give up our children; we just want it to be easier.

Before we knew that our meltdowns were a common, if unsung, occurrence, all we could do was comfort each other. "Think of it this way," I said calmly to Jason, as if I had not been a weepy basket case myself just a week before. "There's no one else in the whole world whose main job it is to watch out for Lily." That really spoke to him and he kissed her on the top of her head, already quietly moving past the terror.

Soon thereafter, a friend insisted that Jason and I go out on a date, leaving Lily with her for the evening—our first time away from the baby in the five weeks we'd had her. People tell stories about how hard it is to leave your baby with the sitter for the first time, but when we handed our precious bundle to our friend, I actually felt calm. We trusted the woman, Lily was likely to sleep through the evening, and I was dying for a date with my husband. As we drove away, it was a little disconcerting, but I was honestly ready to be footloose and formula-free for an evening.

Thinking we needed lighthearted and distracting fare, we settled on a showing of the movie *March of the Penguins*. A nature documentary about adorable little creatures wearing tuxedos on their icebergs, it would be sweet, right? We chose poorly. Unfortunately, the filmmakers were going for a "cycle of life" motif, which meant the sections of the movie were How Penguin Moms Can Die, How Penguin Dads Can Die, How Fetal Penguins Can Die Before Hatching, and How Baby Penguins Can Die If They Live Past That, with subsections like Watch Mother Penguin Cry for Her Frozen Baby and Death Swoops Down from Above. Long before this mortality smorgasbord was over, we were done. Yes, we knew that our diminished physical states and heightened emotions were the real culprits in our shared aversion to the film, but that didn't change the fact that the movie left us both desperate to see our baby. We had been encouraged to stay out as long as we liked that night, but all we really wanted was to hold our girl and protect her from any stray arctic seal or albatross that might come her way. We picked her up at eight o'clock and, happy to do it, headed home together.

Things change. Once you know how to love a baby who can't yet demonstrably return the favor, it's all cream after that, as each developmental milestone rewards you for your patience. When Lily was six weeks old, Jason had her on his lap in the sunroom when I came home from a rare trip out. As I walked into her view, she looked at me and smiled. A real smile, first one dimple flashing and then the other. As long as I live, I'll never forget how that felt. This was no blob; this was a baby. Our baby. She had her Daddy and her Papa, and not only could she now see and recognize us, she could let us know we made her happy.

I'd heard before, of course, that there's nothing like the first time your baby really smiles at you (without it just being a sign of gas). Linda had been telling us for weeks that this was a moment to look forward to. "It's the best," she'd assured us. "The absolute best." As it turns out, she was right.

15

In This Together

WE WERE SUPPOSED TO BE A TWO-DAD FAMILY, BUT THE fact of the matter is I became a total mom. I say that premised on all sorts of stereotypical mom definitions, which is bad form, I know, but considering I have just assigned a mom a penis, I hardly think I'm being too strict in my gender conformity. Yes, I'm male, and I swear there was no breastfeeding, but something about me struck people as specifically maternal. Every adoptive family is visited by a post-placement social worker, and ours, Susan, was the first to actually point out my motherliness aloud. During a home visit that was part of our finalization process, she recalled an expectant woman who had considered picking Jason and me even before Bella matched with us. When that woman found out that she was having a girl, she went with a straight couple because she wanted to be sure there was a mother. "She passed you over for a family with a mom," Susan said, shaking her head. "But just look at Lily—she got a mom anyway." I would have protested that I didn't know what she meant, but I was too busy finishing the hem on a holiday jumper for Lily's visit to Santa.

Honestly, that fall I had come to think of myself as much more momlike than dadlike, and for good reason. Lily had begun daycare three days a week, remaining home with me on the remaining days. At first, spending ten or twelve straight hours alone with a preverbal being had been deeply anxiety producing. No one to hand the baby to when I needed a bathroom break. No one to offer a second opinion as to the relative bulginess of the fontanelle—that terrifying open spot in the top of a baby's skull, which I was sure existed solely to freak me out. No one to plug in the hair dryer when Lily was so overstimulated that only very loud white noise could soothe her. But then I discovered a moms' group.

Arlington, where fertility Gods hold their Olympic games, is so plumped up with stay-at-home mothers that you cannot enter a coffee shop or restaurant during midday hours without stepping over strollers and diaper bags. Among the many resources for all these women was the moms' group at a local church, which a friend of ours—also a new parent—told us about. Unfortunately, when we called to see if I could attend, the person who took the call hemmed and hawed, wondering whether my presence might disrupt all the breastfeeding talk. Instead of answering me outright, she suggested I go to a gay parents' group in another town. Beyond the fact that I am a pedestrian who would have had to take Lily on two buses and two trains to get to that meeting, I was a little put off at the thought of being asked to leave my own community just so that I could hang out with other homos. I already knew how to be gay, thank you; what I really needed was help being a parent.

But then I heard the good news: each moms' group meeting was followed by a baby-buggy migration, in which ten or fifteen of the exhausted souls headed for a local café. I didn't have to go to the meeting; I just had to get my ass to the coffee shop before the last seat was full, which I did. I popped Lily in her baby Bjorn and entered a whole new world—one where I found myself quite at home. Over coffee and sandwiches, a dozen moms at a time rocked their babies like an elaborate perpetual motion machine, as they compared notes, gossiped, and offered free group therapy to each other. They welcomed me without a blink of an eye; with a baby strapped to me in the middle of the day, I had all the credentials I needed for belonging.

At that first lunch, when I asked whether I really needed to take Lily's binky away by four months, as one evil childcare expert had instructed, a dozen binkies appeared around the table as my fellow moms urged me to ignore the (insert expletive here) experts. When another mom asked if anyone knew how to soothe an overtired baby, I offered our hair dryer solution, which spawned a series of other suggestions about the magical properties of sundry vacuums and washing machines. It was like stumbling onto a tribe that spoke my new language.

As the weeks passed, Lily made new playmates and so did her papa. After years without a real work community, I suddenly had a whole raft of diverse friends united by parenthood, among them a geophysicist, a corporate financial consultant, a librarian, and two public schoolteachers. Like me, they were hardly the stereotypical moms of the past, but also like me, they wrestled day to day with the same basic childcare struggles which had faced generations before us. Knowing that these moms were dealing with the same things I was meant I didn't have to go crazy, or at least not for long and not in any spectacular fashion. And I was glad to pass on what I learned from my fellow moms when our friends Ben and Abby finally welcomed their baby, Ruby, eight months after we brought Lily home.

But if I was a mom in some regards, I discovered I was not a wife. I do not want to suggest that any of my new friends were unhappy with their husbands, and indeed, they all seemed very content. At the same time, one of the standard mom topics in the early months was the imbalance in childcare. Husbands, as I kept hearing, were likely to work long hours, calling at the last minute to say they needed just one more meeting or had to have a drink with the boss. Tell a woman who has been alone with a four-month-old since dawn that you need just a little more time, and you might as well throw a bucket of mud in her face: yes, she'll live, but she'll be cursing you for a good long while.

Other husbandly sins included letting clients call the house at all hours, regardless of how long it takes to get a baby to sleep and how a sudden shrill noise is the last thing you want to hear. And then there was the male deployment of that old saw about how a mom can hardly expect a guy who's worked all day to take the baby off her hands. I mean, *come on*.

And those were just the *husband* behaviors. As dads, the poor guys engendered a separate series of complaints. Dads, I was told, claim they understand the no-TV rule set by many moms, but then forget in cases of football, baseball, basketball, and boredom. While dads have the physical capacity to hear a howling cry in the night, they seem to believe that moms, used to getting up for feedings anyway, must thus be better suited to solving nocturnal crises, leaving the dads free to remain in bed. Worse, dads have a terrible predisposition toward Selective Object Blindness (SOB). That is, when it's his turn to watch the baby, giving mom a rare nap or precious evening off, his inner SOB kicks in. He cannot find any number of objects that he needs—wipes, or baby Orajel, or a pacifier—until Mom, pulled away from her leisure, invariably finds the lost item on the changing table right where it is always, *always* kept.

But if there is one thing you don't want to say at a moms' group, it is this: my husband *never* does that! It seemed much more convivial to fall silent, letting the complaints swell around me and subside, knowing that other, safer topics would soon fill up the majority of the conversation. There was at least one mom who, like me, never contributed to the husband-bashing, and she admitted to me in whispers that it was because the stories didn't apply. "I don't want to gloat," she says, "so I keep my mouth shut." I was with her. Every complaint I had heard made me feel like I had won the jackpot with my choice of husband and dad.

Jason always made sure to come home as soon as possible at the end of the workday, and if he needed to run an errand, he'd call first to make sure I wasn't at a point where a straightjacket was needed. On weekends, he would take primary care of Lily so that I could catch up on the work missed because of the days I had her at home. And at night, we worked out a feeding time-share, with shifts so that one or the other of us could get a solid four hours sleep at a stretch. (Four hours does not sound like a lot until you have lived on two hours, and then it seems like heaven.) He shared in every task on the spectrum, from reading the book *Olivia* at bedtime to the less enjoyable application of baby suppositories. And he knew where everything was as well as I did, except maybe items of clothing, which he would find by digging around until her dresser drawers were a mess. But hey, if he was willing to be a poop inducer, I could forgive a sloppy stack of onesies.

I realize that my description of my innate momosity and Jason's great dadness may paint too glossy a picture of our daily lives, not to mention making us sound bizarrely retro—just pearls and a vagina away from the 1950s *Donna Reed Show*. But we had challenges of our own. Not surprisingly, parenting gave us a new forum in which to display our opposing impulses about money. Primarily, these boiled down to Jason Saving for a House and Dave Shopping for a Baby Girl.

Shopping for a Baby Girl, as some of Lily's other fans can tell you, is addictive. Look at a kids' department in a clothing store and you might see four or five burgundy and navy rugby shirts for boys, hanging way off to one side of the fifty spot-lit racks devoted just to little dresses, separates, ensembles, and accessories in dozens of colors, spanning a host of aesthetics. Want to dress your daughter like a twenty-inch country club matron? There's a sweater set with her name on it. Want her to rock the playground in funky style? Grab that adorable crocheted poncho and some bell-bottoms. Think Britney Spears is a positive influence? There are midriff tops for the diaper set. (Pardon me while I shudder.) I found myself helpless before the baby equivalent of cheap chic: a seventies-style jumper adorned with freaky woodland creatures and a leopard-collar jacket that screamed "daughter of the tsar."

But even if I was shopping with my bargain gene intact, each purchase still meant I was spending, not saving, money.

Jason pointed out that Lily had more clothes than either of us. He reminded me that Shopping for a Baby Girl was also the prerogative of grandmothers and aunties, who were doing just fine at no cost to us. He was right and I knew it, but I still hated to stop. Getting to pick out clothes for Lily myself, instead of just dressing her in other people's picks, was just too enticing. My fellow moms backed me up on this. When I mentioned the debate to one mom on a playdate, she ran into her bedroom and returned with three outfits she had purchased for her boy, knowing that her husband was going to make her return two of them. Yet another friend from the group told me that her husband suggested they just cut the feet off a sleeper their son had outgrown, in hopes of getting more use out of the mutilated garment.

Eventually, I slowed down my Shopping for a Baby Girl—I am not completely without fiscal reason, after all—but that didn't mean I completely gave up on wielding influence over what Lily wore. I whipped out needle and thread and focused on altering existing items to suit my taste—you know, cutting the legs off overalls and hemming the remaining material into a little dress, or turning fat-baby pants into a jaunty winter hat. *That* sort of thing.

While my husband was trying to rein me in financially, I was having to ride herd on him emotionally. This was a reversal of a decade-old pattern. My nondemonstrative, drama-avoiding pragmatist had lost his mind. I exaggerate, but parenthood had tripped several triggers in Jason's psyche, rewiring his emotions. On the plus side, he became a guy who cried when touched by a story or memory; this development galled him, but I lapped it up. On the down side, he also developed a paranoid ability to imagine terrible scenarios for the future. He became the family's default awfulizer, wondering aloud if a cough meant cystic fibrosis, and spending way too much time figuring out how to prepare for bird flu.

When Lily learned to sit up and preferred to play that way, he worried she'd never again roll over or learn to crawl or move from the spot she occupied like a potted plant. When she began to coo but wasn't using any consonants, he worried that she wasn't truly babbling. If she seemed hot to the touch, or even just not cold, he'd beg me to take her temperature, even if he had already done so himself. I found myself in an unlikely position: I had to be the calming one, the husband who said things like, "Yes, someday she will use her legs" or "If we take her temperature for a fifth time today, she's going to grow up with a serious anal fixation and it *will* be our fault." Parenthood had transformed us in a completely unexpected way: for once in our lives, I had to be the guy with his feet on the ground.

We were not the only ones transformed by Lily's arrival. Our mothers were now all grandmothers, and they blossomed in their new roles. Nancy, Jason's mom, was now Grammy Nan and she took such delight in her new granddaughter that she managed to overcome her aversion to the city (as she and all our relatives thought of Arlington, a town of fewer than 50,000 people). Though still refusing to engage Boston drivers on the highway, which is understandable for a woman who lives in rural New Hampshire, she braved the tedium of two-hour bus rides so that she could be the first grandmother to see Lily sit up, stand, and pop a tooth through.

Linda was not old enough to ever have seemed like a mother figure to Jason, even though she was married to his dad, and I

felt much more like her friend than her son-in-law. But she became Nana Linda effortlessly, and her mother Gerry instantly
assumed the role of Lily's doting only great-grandmother. Even
living far away in Michigan, Nana Linda reveled in the chance
to shower Lily with clothing, wisely staying ahead of the seemingly nonstop growth spurts. When Jason asked Linda to slow
down the deliveries, thinking the resources might be used better
elsewhere, she took umbrage, pointing out that he was killing
her *naches*, the joy a grandparent gets from a grandchild. And
when we made a trip to Michigan to see that side of the family,
Lily took to Linda so quickly that at one crowded family gathering, when relatives swarmed around, she looked to her Nana
Linda for comfort as often as she looked to us.

But perhaps the most profound transformation was that of
my mother. Despite our true closeness, something we've nurtured with conversations every single Saturday morning since I
left for religious boarding school at sixteen, we have never had
an uncomplicated relationship. After all, she missed my wedding, which she disapproved of; she still believed, despite years
of enjoying our love and support, that Jason and I would be
eternally lost if we never renounced our homosexuality; and
she had not originally expressed much enthusiasm about our
adopting. But then came Lily, who completely captured Mom's
heart.

Living four hours away and being physically unwell, my
mom hadn't actually met Lily, but she quickly became Grammy
Jo nonetheless. Every picture we sent and every story we told
was treasured. Living on social security as she does, she never
has a dime to spare. For many holidays, she can't afford to
send cards as she'd like to and apologizes, even though anyone
who knows her understands. But Lily was too precious to her,

and she went to the nearest Wal-Mart, spending the few dollars she had on a fleece blanket and stuffed cow with a blinking nose. These were simple gifts, but they brought to mind the biblical story of the widow's two mites: when you give all you have, it's more dear.

We had intended for Mom to meet Lily at Thanksgiving, but a blizzard cancelled our trip. Lily was six months old and Grammy Jo still hadn't seen her. The next weekend, despite more snow, we decided to make the trip anyway. We were both tense; the drive always took four hours, but it felt even longer as it was Lily's first trip trapped in a car seat for that length of time. When we hit a traffic jam just outside the city, barely crawling for an hour, we almost turned back. But, for my mom's sake, we knew we needed to get the baby up there before too much more time had passed, and we drove on.

My mom lit up when she saw Lily. I hadn't seen her look so pleased in years. And to my surprise, considering the general physical discomfort she lived with from lupus and a half dozen other chronic ailments, she asked if she could hold the baby on her lap. In typical fashion, Lily took in this new grandmother with a long dark look, then decided it was safe and reached for Grammy Jo's eyeglasses. At one point, my mom leaned in and whispered to her, "You are my Christmas. Yes, you are."

As we drove home that night, I cried all the way to the freeway. I had thought the visit was for my mom's benefit. It had never occurred to me how much I needed to see my mother and my daughter together for my own sake. I had longed to see my families—the one I came from and the one I chose—emotionally united in a way that hadn't happened on my wedding day, and now I had. I know it's not easy to unlearn a belief, especially one long held, but I'd like to think that seeing her beautiful granddaughter gave Mom reason to reconsider just how God might feel about the dads who'd been chosen to raise Lily.

With our relatives more connected to us than ever, our old friends welcoming Lily with open arms, and our new friends helping us figure out what the hell we were doing, we were fully immersed in one of those villages that Hillary Clinton famously cites as being needed to raise a child. That kind of support makes a difference in a million ways, and I often wonder how a parent living alone ever pulls it off.

But at the same time, when it came right down to it, in the dark of a long night when the baby was coughing and crying, it was just me and the man I love on the front lines. As we swapped shifts of soothing the baby and took turns making her bottle at 1:00 a.m. while the other changed her diaper, we found that the middle of the night was a great time to see what our marriage was made of—and we liked the unified image we saw.

Trips to the emergency room can have a similar uniting effect on a family. Our social worker had told me that some adoptive families actually need the crisis of the first illness to bond. We were plenty bonded already, thank you, but somehow that didn't spare us from having hospital runs. Once, Lily caught a cold, not a shocking thing for a baby to do, which made her nose run and her temperature rise. After half-jokingly ruling out eastern equine encephalitis and scarlet fever, we followed the standard parent-as-doctor routine of giving her Tylenol, sucking snot out of her nose with a little bulb thing, and steaming her in the shower like a dumpling. But on the second day of this particular cold, Lily turned bright red and began to give off heat like a furnace. In baby care lore, two days of a fever is no big whoop, so we tried to play it as cool as our personalities allowed. On the third day, her fever rose to 103.9, which seemed freakishly high to us, but not to the pediatric nurse we called. It wasn't especially worrisome in an infant, she assured us, as long as it was accompanied by no other symptoms. On the fourth day, at the doctor's office, our pediatrician told us that a harmless little virus was going around but she wasn't too concerned, as long as Lily wasn't coughing.

Two hours after leaving the doctor's office, the coughs began. By bedtime, Lily's coughing had become so frequent and fierce that each cough was followed by a cry of pain. Jason and I split the night, taking turns sleeping in Lily's room to comfort her. It required no awfulizing to see that our baby was not doing well.

The next day, I made a second appointment with the doctor. By the time we got there, Lily had pretty much stopped eating or wetting her diapers. When our doctor opened Lily's shirt and saw that each breath pulled the skin of Lily's chest tight against her ribs, the doctor shook her head, amazed at how quickly Lily had gone downhill. This wasn't a problem that she could solve by sending us off with a prescription. It was off to the emergency room instead.

Lily's cold had become bronchiolitis, which is like a painful infant version of bronchitis, and had quickly worsened into pneumonia. It was a terrible thing to see the IV taped to her tiny arm to keep her hydrated, and every test made her cry as hard as she could with her partly sealed lungs. As freaked out as we had been all week at home before this, finally knowing what was wrong and having people caring for Lily was an immense relief. A kind of calm prevailed: Jason and I made plans as to which one of us would stay the first night at the hospital and who would stay the next; we canceled classes or moved appointments so we could be there for Lily; and we arranged with our neighbor to keep an eye on Sasha while we were out. We'd always done best when we were working as a team toward a common goal, and there had never been a task we were more invested in than this. We knew that, in the grand scheme of things, a little pneumonia isn't the worst crisis new parents have ever faced, so instead of being terrorized by the sudden hospitalization, we just dug in being the best dads we could be. Within hours of her first treatment in the hospital, Lily's fever began to drop and she showed interest in a bottle again. Soon enough, she was fine.

Because Lily, we learned, had asthma, this would be only one of three hospital stays in the first year of her life. Since we kept checking in, we jokingly began to refer to the hospital as our hotel. This was the scene of one of my favorite memories of parenthood so far: I walked into Lily's hospital room after Jason had spent the night with her there, and I found him sitting up in the crib, holding Lily. Jason's no contortionist, mind you—this was not a bassinette, but a big metal kid's bed with criblike rails. I could see for myself that it was large enough for a worried dad to share with his baby, but I had never imagined doing such a thing until I walked into the room and saw them sitting in it together.

In a moment, time slipped away: all those years before, Jason had done the same thing to comfort me after my surgery; his presence had calmed me then, and it calmed Lily now. Despite the slender tubes and wires protruding from one small arm and her tiny foot, Lily was cuddled contentedly in her

Daddy's lap. "Everything I love best in the world is in that bed," I thought to myself, though I didn't say it aloud. I didn't need to; Jason just shot me one of his I-know-you're-being-sentimental looks, and rolled his eyes. He turned Lily around so she could see me. "It's Papa," he said, and she flashed her new one-tooth smile.

I scooped my daughter up, gave my husband a kiss, and started another day with my family.

Acknowledgments

~

Thanks to . . .

My writing teachers: Ann Parrish, Mary Norcliffe, Betsy Carpenter, and Marcie Hershman. Editors who allowed me a voice for increasingly larger audiences: Jeff Epperly (drama and all) and Rudy Kikel at *Bay Windows*; the unmatched Susan Ryan Vollmar at the *Boston Phoenix*; Doug Most, Suzanne Althoff, and Anne V. Nelson at the *Boston Globe*; and Da Capo's Wendy Holt, the kind of editor who makes a writer glad to be a writer. Those who have supported my work with cash as well as development: The Theater Offensive (big smooches), Ensemble Studio Theatre, and the Alfred P. Sloan Foundation. People who help keep families like mine safe and supported: Mary Bonuato, Mass Equality, and GLAD. People who bring families together: Janet, Betsy, Susan, Carol, Marty, and Anne of Adoption Resources of Jewish Family & Children's Service of Greater Boston; Lisa, Jennifer, and Amy at the Midwestern adoption agency. And the people who make up the village surrounding my child: my husband, Lily's birth mom, our terrifically supportive families, our loving friends, and my fellow moms, with their husbands and kids, in Arlington, Massachusetts, where families come in as many forms as there are constellations and shine just as brightly.